Oxford
International
Resources

7

# Skills
## Problem Solving and Reasoning

Karen Morrison
Lisa Greenstein

OXFORD

**OXFORD**
UNIVERSITY PRESS

Great Clarendon Street, Oxford, OX2 6DP, United Kingdom

Oxford University Press is a department of the University of Oxford.
It furthers the University's objective of excellence in research, scholarship, and education by publishing worldwide. Oxford is a registered trade mark of Oxford University Press in the UK and in certain other countries.

British Library Cataloguing in Publication Data
Data available

9781382045643

10 9 8 7 6 5 4 3 2 1

Paper used in the production of this book is a natural, recyclable product made from wood grown in sustainable forests.

The manufacturing process conforms to the environmental regulations of the country of origin.

Printed in China by Golden Cup

**Acknowledgements**
The publisher and authors would like to thank the following for permission to use photographs and other copyright material:

**Photos: p8:** dmitrimaruta / 123RF; **p9:** Rei Imagine / Shutterstock; **p10:** naka-stockphoto / Shutterstock; **p12:** Christina Richards / Shutterstock; **p14:** Just Life / Shutterstock; **p15:** Sharon Day / Shutterstock; **p17:** Pack / Shutterstock; **p18:** elenabsl / Shutterstock; **p23(t):** RAUL ARBOLEDA / Contributor / Getty; **p23(b):** Singkham / Shutterstock; **p24:** tykhyi © 123RF.com; **p27:** maniraja / Shutterstock; **p28:** Jason Prince / Shutterstock; **p30:** Geza Kurka_Hungary / Shutterstock; **p36:** Bilal Hafeez3249 / Shutterstock; **p40:** Holli / Shutterstock; **p41(t):** Benny Marty / Shutterstock; **p41(b):** kikujungboy CC / Shutterstock; **p42(l):** efe_madrid / © Freepik Company; **p42(r), 76(e):** The Print Collector / Alamy Stock Photo; **p44:** Eman Kazemi / Alamy Stock Photo; **p50:** Olga Popova / Shutterstock; **p51:** Svitlana_Shepitsena / Shutterstock; **p54:** Arto Hakola / Shutterstock; **p55(tl):** Traveller MG / Shutterstock; **p55(tr):** Dilomski / Shutterstock; **p55(bl):** Brian E Kushner / Shutterstock; **p55(br):** pandapaw / Shutterstock; **p56:** Nature Picture Library / Alamy Stock Photo; **p57:** Roy F Wylam / Shutterstock; **p58(t):** Ludmila Smite / 123RF; **p58(mt):** Pierre Watson / Shutterstock; **p58(mb):** Michal Pesata / Shutterstock; **p58(b):** Rosalie Kreulen / Shutterstock; **p60:** Hemis / Alamy Stock Photo; **p62:** GUDKOV ANDREY / Shutterstock; **p64:** Ethan Daniels / Shutterstock; **p65:** David Ashley / Shutterstock; **p66, 68:** mavo / Shutterstock; **p70(t):** MTZKT / Shutterstock; **p70(ml):** Lana Iva / Shutterstock; **p70(mr):** tescha555 / Shutterstock; **p70(b):** Athawit Ketsak / Shutterstock; **p71(l):** Bettina Calder / Shutterstock; **p71(r):** Vladimir Mulder / Shutterstock; **p72, 78:** Peter Wollinga / Shutterstock; **p74:** Sivakova Valeria / Shutterstock; **p75:** DenisProduction.com / Shutterstock; **p76(a):** Satoshi.RR / Shutterstock; **p76(b):** Nastasic / Getty; **p76(c):** Peter Horree / Alamy Stock Photo; **p76(d):** Kypros / Getty.

**Cover art:** Andrea Manzati

**Artwork by:** Q2A Media, Katya Balakina, Andrew Painter, Eva Sassin, Julissa Mora, Peter Stevenson, Sam Ward, Steve Cox and Oxford University Press.

Every effort has been made to contact copyright holders of material reproduced in this book. Any omissions will be rectified in subsequent printings if notice is given to the publisher.

Links to third party websites are provided by Oxford in good faith and for information only. Oxford disclaims any responsibility for the materials contained in any third party website referenced in this work.

MIX
Paper | Supporting responsible forestry
FSC™ C110497
www.fsc.org

# Contents

# My problem-solving record

These are the steps I follow to solve a problem...

**1** **Read and understand the problem** → **2** **Choose a strategy**

These are the strategies I tried...

Guess, check and improve

Draw a diagram

Work back from what I know

Use equations, formulae or ratios

| 1 | 2 | 3 | 4 | 5 | 6 |
|---|---|---|---|---|---|
|   |   |   |   |   |   |

|   | 1 |
|---|---|
|   | 2 |
|   | 3 |
|   | 4 |
|   | 5 |
|   | 6 |

4

Make connections

① ② ③ ④ ⑤ ⑥

Use data and work systematically

| 1 | 2 | 3 | 4 | 5 | 6 |
|---|---|---|---|---|---|
|   |   |   |   |   |   |

Consider different cases or a simpler version of the problem

| 1 | 2 | 3 | 4 | 5 | 6 |
|---|---|---|---|---|---|

Use logical reasoning

| 1 | 4 |
|---|---|
| 2 | 5 |
| 3 | 6 |

## Think, talk, solve

A school holds an annual Walkathon to raise money for charity. Read the poster for the event.

**Take part in Hillcrest School's annual**

**WALK-A-THON**

**FUNDRAISER**

| Group | A | B | C |
|---|---|---|---|
| Ages | 6–8 | 9–11 | 12–14 |
| Route distance | 700 m | 1.4 km | 2.1 km |

**How to take part**

- Find your group in the table! Each age group has a different route to walk or run.
- Ask members of the community, family and friends to **sponsor** you.
- Ask your sponsors to **pledge** an amount of money for each time that you complete the route.
- On the day of Walkathon, complete the route as many times as you can in 1 hour.

**1** True or false? Explain how you decided.

**a** Group A's route is half as long as Group B's route.

_____

**b** Group C's route is double Group B's route.

_____

**c** The route distances can be expressed in the ratio 1:2:3.

_____

**2** Teresa has ten sponsors, who make these pledges:  £2  £5  £3.50 £2  £4  £8 £3  £2  £5  £2

**a** What is the **mean** of this set of pledges? _____

**b** Write an easy **formula** that Teresa can use to calculate the total amount she will raise. Use $n$ for the number of times she completes the route.

_____

**c** On the day of the Walkathon, Teresa completed the route 3 times. How much money did she raise?

**d** Teresa is in group C. Work out how much money she raised per kilometre.

## Let's reason ...

This graph shows the number of times that the students in each group completed their route.

**3 a** What type of graph is this? Circle the best option. Give a reason for your choice.

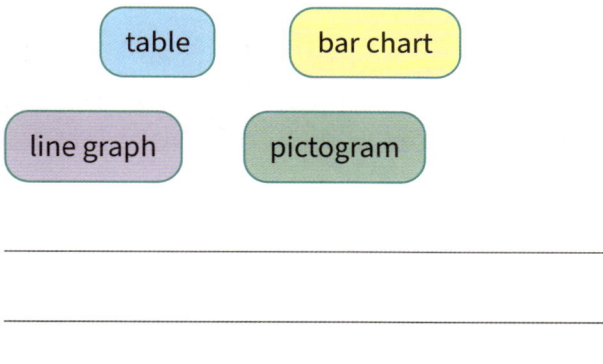

_____

_____

_____

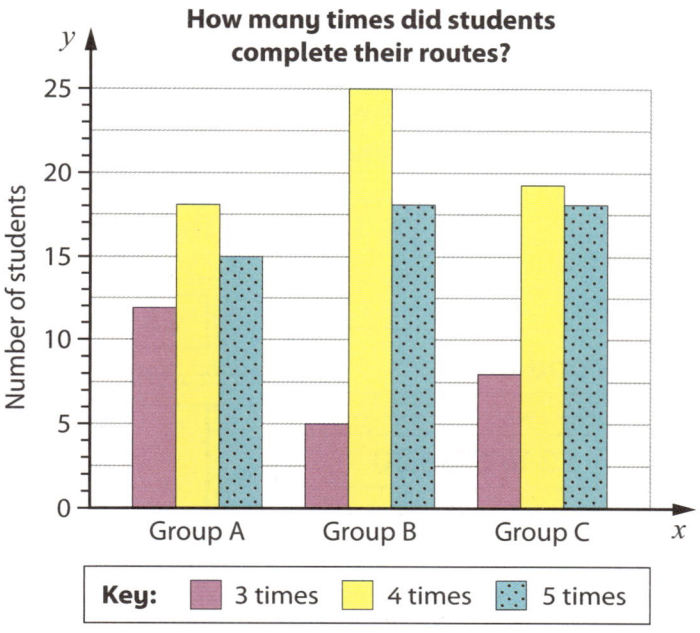

**b** Explain in your own words what the graph compares.

_____

_____

**4** Use the graph to work out the total number of students in each group.

**5** Identify a **trend** or pattern that was the same across all three groups.

_____

_____

_____

**6** Discuss the trends you noticed with other students in the class.

## Think, talk, solve

A radio station raises money for charities. They invite their listeners to phone the station and make **donations**. These are the amounts they collected for two different charities.

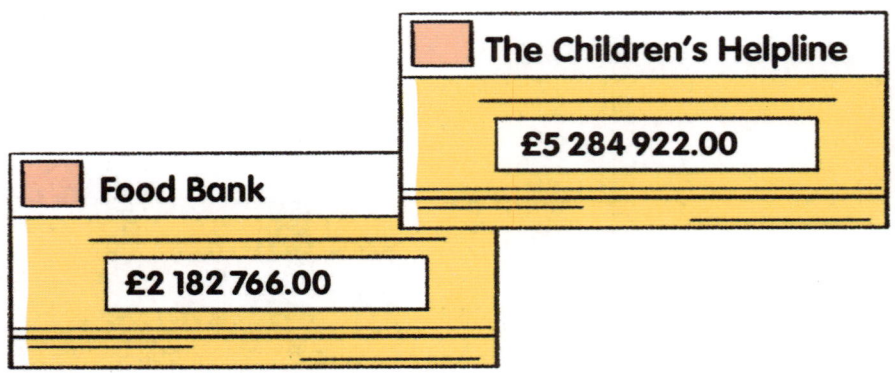

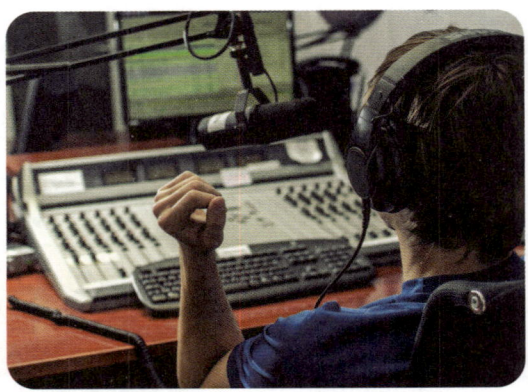

1 The digit 2 occurs five times in the amounts on the cheques. Write what each 2 represents.

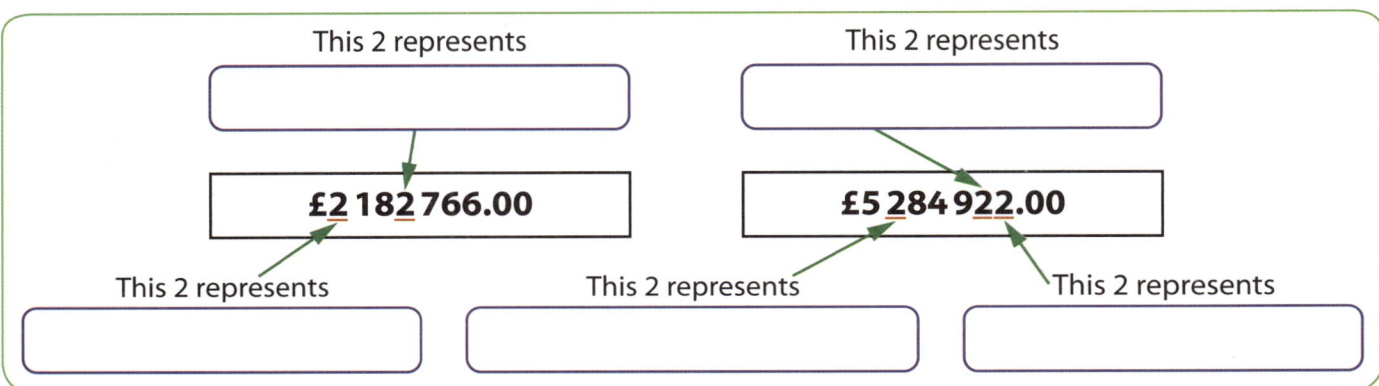

| This 2 represents | | This 2 represents |
| --- | --- | --- |
| | | |

£2 182 766.00        £5 284 922.00

| This 2 represents | This 2 represents | This 2 represents |
| --- | --- | --- |
| | | |

2 a How much did the two charities receive altogether?

b How much more did The Children's Helpline receive than the Food Bank?

3 The radio station has a total fundraising target of £10 000 000 for the year.
How much more do they have to raise to reach this target?

### Let's solve …

**4** Before the Food Bank received the donation, it was in **debt**. Its bank balance was −£475 675.00.

   **a** The Food Bank manager wants to know the bank balance after receiving the donation. Circle the calculation she <u>cannot</u> use to calculate the balance.

> −£475 675.00 + £2 182 766.00

> £2 182 766.00 − £475 675.00

> £2 182 766.00 − (−£475 675.00)

   **b** Explain your thinking.

_____

**5** Check your reasoning from question 4. Work out the Food Bank's bank balance after receiving the donation.

**6** One anonymous donor gave three-quarters of a million pounds to the fundraiser for The Children's Helpline. The rest of the money was from other donors.

   **a** How much money did the other donors give?

   **b** The mean amount of money given by the other donors was £15. Approximately how many other donors were there?

   **c** What percentage of the total did the other donors contribute? Round your percentage to the nearest whole number.

_____

_____

**7** In many cultures, people prefer to give donations anonymously. Discuss with a partner the reasons for this.

1  When The Children's Helpline applied to the radio station for a donation, they gave this summary of their monthly expenses to show that they needed help.

| Monthly income | |
| --- | --- |
| Donations | £10 000.00 |
| Government grants | £5000.00 |
| Fundraising events | £3000.00 |

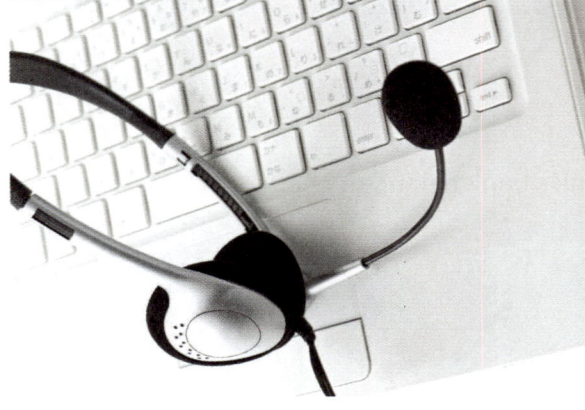

| Monthly expenses | | |
| --- | --- | --- |
| **1. Salaries and wages** | | |
| Call centre staff | £8000 | **£12 500** |
| Administrative staff | £3500 | |
| Volunteer costs | £1000 | |
| **2. Operations and infrastructure** | | |
| Rent and utilities | £2500 | **£3300** |
| Telephone and internet | £500 | |
| Office supplies | £300 | |
| **3. Marketing and outreach work** | | |
| Marketing and advertising | £1000 | **£1500** |
| Community engagement | £500 | |
| **4. Training and development** | | |
| Training courses | £800 | **£1000** |
| Materials | £200 | |
| **5. Miscellaneous expenses** | | |
| Insurance | £500 | **£600** |
| Bank fees | £100 | |

a  The Children's Helpline runs at a loss. Calculate the monthly loss and write it as a negative number.

Running at a loss means that the charity's expenses are greater than its income, so the charity makes a negative amount of money each month.

b  At the beginning of the year The Children's Helpline has a positive bank balance of £3900. It runs at the same monthly loss for a whole year. What is the charity's bank balance at the end of the year?

## Let's solve …

**2** Sometimes we need to simplify fractions to make them easier to work with. These examples show how two different students simplified their fractions.

$\frac{12\,000}{15\,000}$ – Cancelling 3 zeros is the same as dividing the numerator and the denominator by 1000.

$= \frac{12}{15}$ – 3 is a factor of 12 and 15.

$= \frac{4}{5}$

$\frac{126}{147}$ I don't know the factors of these numbers, so I use the rules of divisibility. I can divide the numerator and the denominator by 3.

$126 \div 3 = 42$

$147 \div 3 = 49$

Now I see they are both multiples of 7.

$42 = 6$ sevens

$49 = 7$ sevens

So $\frac{126}{147} = \frac{6}{7}$

Express each of the charity's five monthly expenses as a fraction of the total expenses. Then simplify the fractions.

**a** Salaries and wages _____

**b** Operations and infrastructure _____

**c** Marketing and outreach work _____

**d** Training and development _____

**e** Miscellaneous expenses _____

**3** Use your calculations to help you draw a pie chart of the charity's expenses.

Remember that a full turn around the centre of a circle is 360°. Convert your fractions so they have a denominator of 360.

## Think, talk, solve

**1** A thrift store (charity shop) receives boxes of shoes and clothing to sell for charity. When the volunteers display the items for sale, they arrange three pairs of shoes around one pair of boots. They follow similar rules for other items.

Complete the tables. Then write the pattern or rule you notice for each set of items.

**a** Boots and shoes

| Pairs of boots | 1 | 2 | 3 | | | |
|---|---|---|---|---|---|---|
| Pairs of shoes | 3 | 4 | 5 | | | |

Rule: _____

**b** Men's shirts and pants

| Shirts | 3 | 6 | 9 | | | |
|---|---|---|---|---|---|---|
| Pants | 2 | 4 | 6 | | | |

Rule: _____

**c** Women's dresses and skirts

| Dresses | 2 | 4 | 6 | | | |
|---|---|---|---|---|---|---|
| Skirts | 1 | 2 | 3 | | | |

Rule: _____

**2** Kayleigh is a volunteer at the thrift store. She wants to write a formula so the other volunteers can easily calculate how many boots and shoes to display together. She tries these three formulae.

Which formula gives the correct number of boots and shoes? Explain how you checked.

$s = 2 \times b$      $s = 2 + b$      $s = b \div 2$

$s$ = number of pairs of shoes
$b$ = number of pairs boots

_____

_____

### Let's reason ...

The thrift store receives a box of scarves. The volunteers wash and dry the scarves before they sell them in the store.

They hang the scarves like this, using three pegs per scarf. The pegs at each end are shared with the next scarf.

**3** Use the picture to help you work out how many pegs the volunteers use for:

   **a** 4 scarves   _____

   **b** 5 scarves   _____

**4** Kayleigh writes this formula to work out the number of pegs needed for any number of scarves. Use the formula to work out how many pegs the volunteers need for:

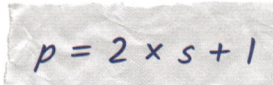

$$p = 2 \times s + 1$$

   **a** 1 scarf   _____

   **b** 6 scarves   _____

   **c** 10 scarves   _____

**5** Look at this information about the benefits that volunteers receive at the thrift store.

### Thrift Store volunteer benefits

Choose **one** of these benefits every shift* you work!
\* Each shift is 3–5 hours long.

**Lunch allowance**
You will receive:
£6 per shift

**Credit tokens** to spend in the thrift store
1 credit = £2
You will receive:
1 free credit per shift, plus half a credit for each full hour worked

Work with a partner. Find a way to compare the two options. Decide which you think is the better option. Write your working and ideas.

## Think, talk, reason

Marco is 8 years old. Marco's Grandpa Leo looks after Marco after school every day from Monday to Friday while Marco's mum is at work. Marco gets home from school at 3:15 p.m. and Marco's mum gets home from work at 6:45 p.m.

If Marco's mum had to pay for childcare, she would pay £11 per hour.

1  How many hours does Grandpa Leo look after Marco:

   a  each day?          _____

   b  each week?         _____

   c  each month?        _____

   > Calculate a month as four weeks.

   d  How much would Marco's mum pay for childcare each month if Grandpa Leo didn't look after Marco?

2  Grandpa Leo is $9\frac{1}{2}$ times Marco's age. Work out how old Grandpa Leo is.

3  Grandpa Leo likes riddles. He gives Marco this riddle to solve about his cousins.

   > Your cousin Margot is a quarter of my age. Your cousin Elsa is half of Margot's age.

   Work out the ages of Marco's cousins.

### Let's solve …

Marco and Grandpa Leo are making a gift for Marco's mum for Mother's Day. It is a bird nesting box. Marco draws this sketch to show the **dimensions**.

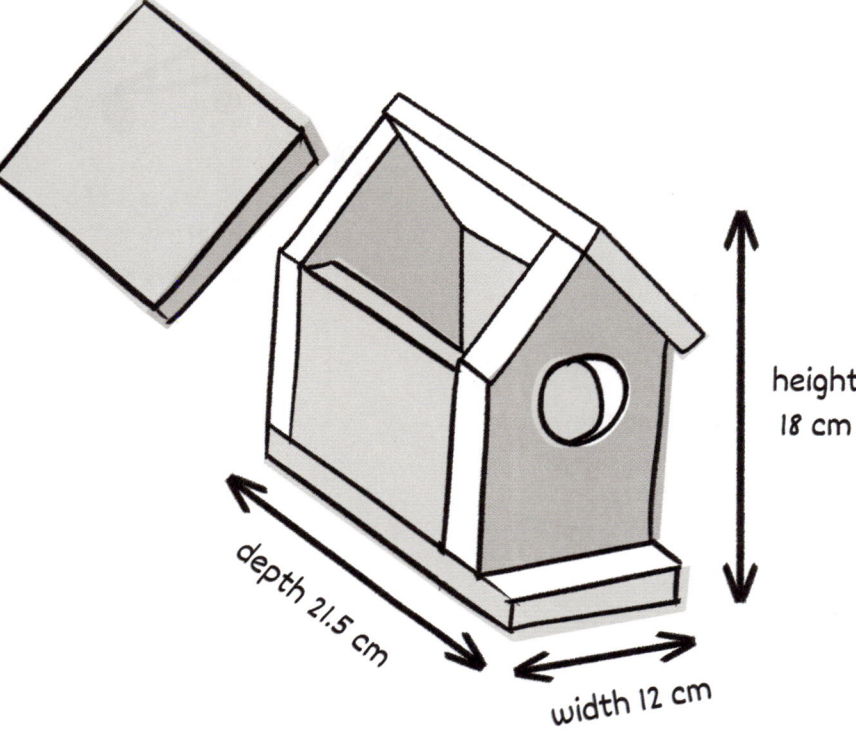

height
18 cm

depth 21.5 cm

width 12 cm

**4** When the bird box is finished, Marco designs a box to put it in. He sketches a net for the box.

Label the net with sensible dimensions for a box that is big enough to hold the bird box. There should be at least 0.5 cm space around each side of the bird box inside the box.

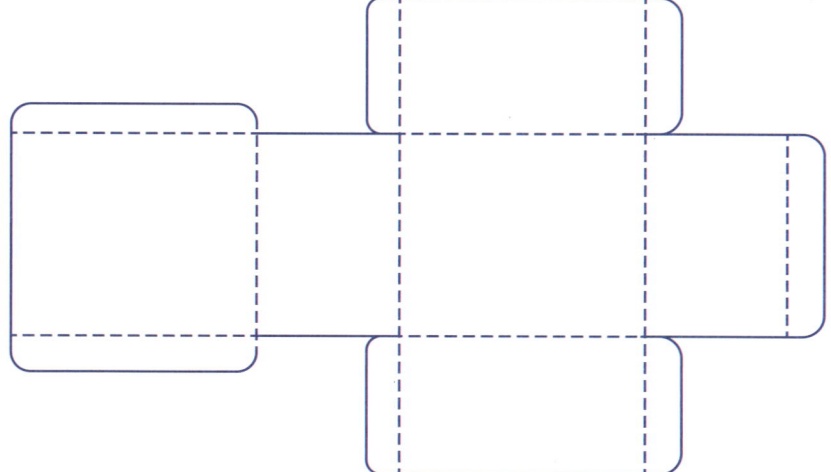

**5** The bird box is made from a length of wood 12 mm thick and 120 mm wide.

 **a** Use rounding and estimation to work out what length of wood Marco needs to make the bird box. Circle your choice.

 **b** Explain how you decided.

$\frac{1}{2}$ m    1 m    1.5 m

### Let's solve ...

Food Bank Donations

During one month, a supermarket collects food donations for the Food Bank. They place a shopping cart at the entrance of the supermarket. Customers can place tins of food and boxes of cereal in the cart. The supermarket has a goal of 1 tonne of food by the end of the month.

**1** A tin contains about 400 g of food. How many tins does the supermarket need to collect to reach its goal of 1 tonne?

Remember,
1 tonne = 1000 kg.

**2** 1 box contains 750 g of cereal. The supermarket thinks that 20% of the total 1 tonne goal will be boxes of cereal. How many boxes is this?

**3** After the first week, the supermarket has collected 32 boxes of cereal and 305 tins.

**a** Work out the total mass of the food collected.

_____

**b** Work out how far the supermarket has progressed towards its goal. Colour the fundraising thermometer to show the progress.

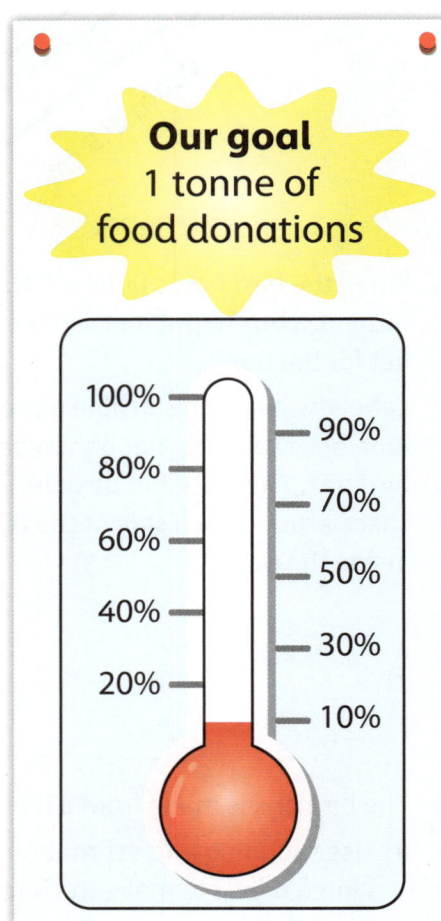

**Our goal**
**1 tonne of food donations**

100% — 90% — 80% — 70% — 60% — 50% — 40% — 30% — 20% — 10%

**c** If customers continue to donate the same amount of food each week, will the supermarket reach its goal by the end of the month? Give reasons for your answer.

_____

_____

Some students volunteer to help to sort the food donations and make food hampers.
Team A and Team B are sorting the tins of food.

**4** Team A arranges their
tins in shapes to make
this pattern.

**a** Describe in words how Team A has arranged the tins.

_____

**b** Draw the next shape in the pattern.

**c** Dayo uses this table to record the number of tins in the pattern.

| Term | 1 | 2 | 3 | 4 | 5 | 6 | 7 | 8 |
|---|---|---|---|---|---|---|---|---|
| **Number of tins in the shape** | 4 | 6 | 8 | 10 | | | | |
| **Total number of tins in the pattern** | 4 | 10 | 18 | 28 | | | | |

Remember, a **term** is a number or shape in a sequence.

Read what Dayo said. What is her mistake?

_____

_____

> I predict that the next number in the bottom row will be 38.

**d** Complete the table to show how many tins Team A will use to make 8 shapes.

**5** Team B arranges their tins in shapes to make
this pattern.
They use this table to record the number of tins
in the pattern.

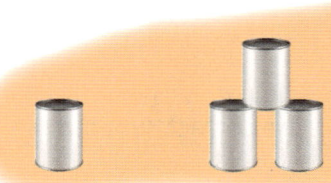

| Term | 1 | 2 | 3 | 4 | 5 | 6 | 7 | 8 |
|---|---|---|---|---|---|---|---|---|
| **Number of tins in the shape** | 1 | 3 | 6 | 10 | | | | |
| **Total number of tins in the pattern** | 1 | 4 | 10 | 20 | | | | |

**a** Without completing the table, discuss with a partner which team is likely to use more tins in their pattern after 8 shapes.

**b** Complete the table. What do you notice? What do you wonder?

➡ Turn back to page 4 and complete the problem-solving record.

### Think, talk, reason

1 Study this chart. Answer the questions with a partner. Write your answers.

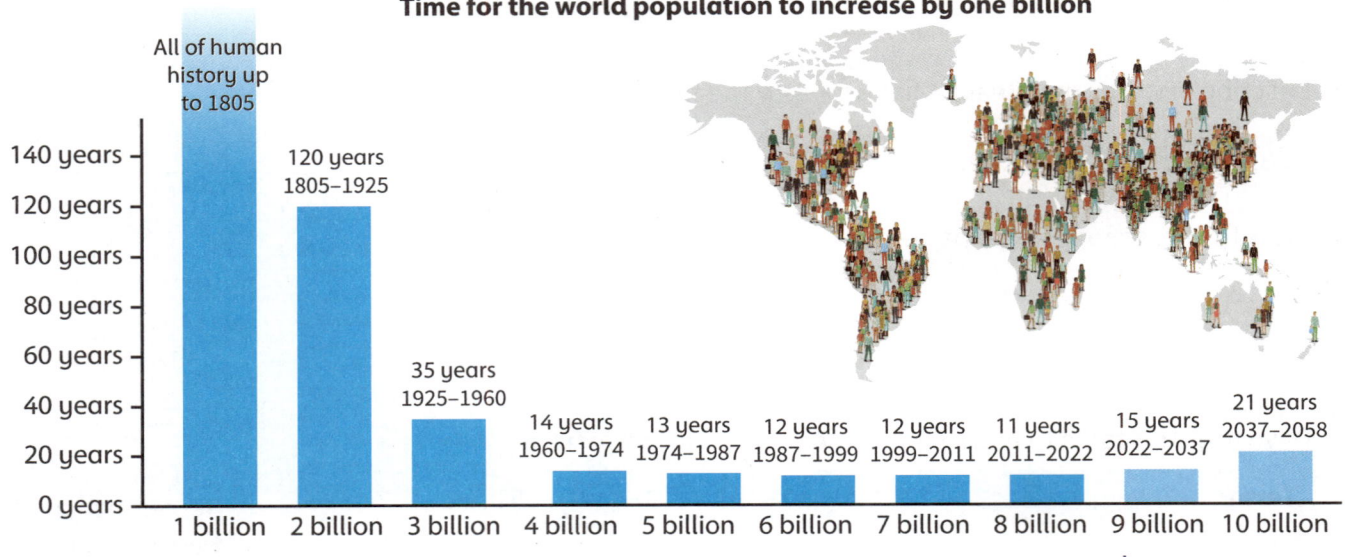

**Time for the world population to increase by one billion**

a Describe the trends shown on the chart.

_____

_____

_____

b The United Nations (UN) estimated that the world population reached 1 billion in 1805 and that it reached 8 billion in 2022. How many years did it take for the population to increase from 1 to 8 billion?

_____

c If the times on the chart are correct, when was the world population 7 billion?

_____

d Based on the UN **projections** shown on the chart, when will the world population reach 9 billion?

_____

e The UN estimates that it will take 15 years for the world population to increase from 8 to 9 billion people. Estimate the world population this year.

_____

**2** As the world's population has grown, the amount of carbon dioxide ($CO_2$) in the atmosphere has increased. $CO_2$ is a greenhouse gas. It traps heat in the Earth's atmosphere, which contributes to global warming.

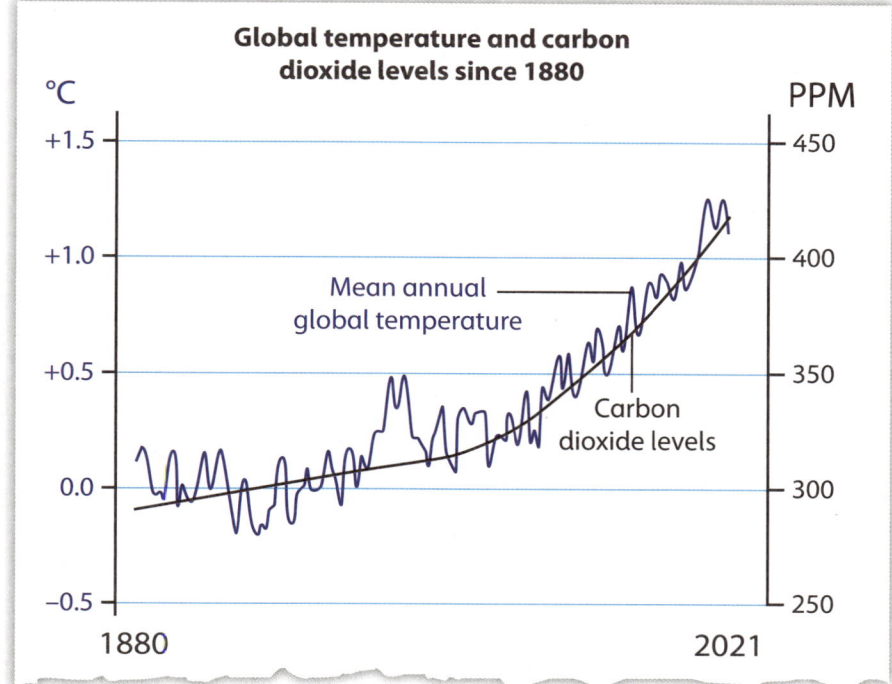

> The $CO_2$ comes from burning fossil fuels, deforestation and some industries.

Answer these questions about the graph.

**a** 1880 is used here as a **baseline**. What do you think that means?

_____

**b** Scientists have collected global temperature data since 1880. In 1880, the mean annual temperature for the whole world was 13.8 °C. Describe in detail how the temperature has changed since then. Include an estimate of the mean annual temperature for the whole world in 2021.

_____

_____

**c** PPM means parts per million. 400 PPM means that there are 400 particles of $CO_2$ in every million particles of air. Express a $CO_2$ level of 418 PPM as a percentage of the air.

_____

**d** Suggest one reason why the temperature line on the graph spikes up and down while the $CO_2$ line is a smoother curve.

_____

_____

We use renewable and non-renewable resources to produce electricity.

**1** The table shows the main sources of electricity that Germany used in 2021.

   **a** Use the blank pie chart outline to show this data visually.

| Resource | % of total |
|---|---|
| Natural gas | 15.3 |
| Nuclear | 11.8 |
| Coal | 28.0 |
| Oil | 0.8 |
| Other non-renewable | 3.2 |
| Renewable resources | 40.9 |

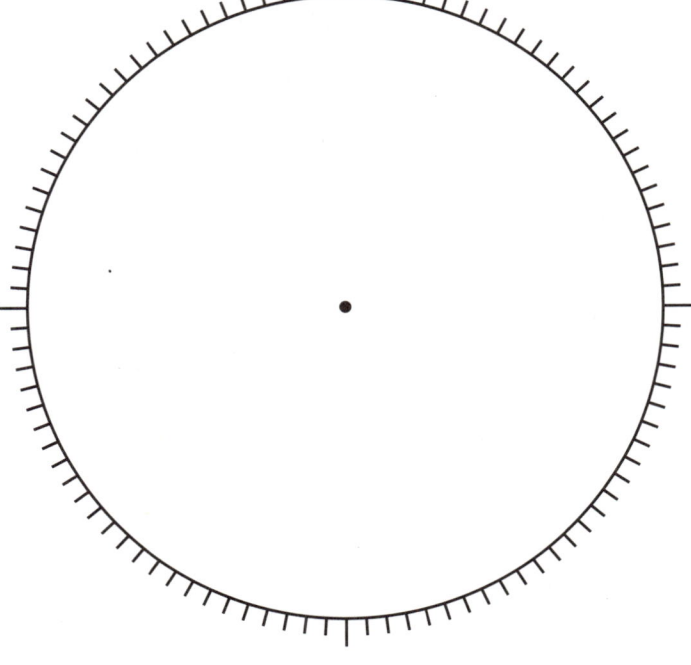

   **b** This table shows how many terawatt hours (TWh) of electricity Germany gets from different renewable resources.

| Resource | Wind | Hydro | Biomass | Solar | Other |
|---|---|---|---|---|---|
| TWh | 117.3 | 19.7 | 43.9 | 51.2 | 5.9 |

    Work with a partner to decide how to add this information to the pie chart above.

A terawatt hour (TWh) is a very large unit used to measure the amount of electricity produced. 1 TWh means 1 trillion watts produced in 1 hour.

**2** 86% of Iceland's electricity comes from renewable resources. 66% of these renewable resources are geothermal resources.

   **a** What percentage of Iceland's total electricity comes from geothermal resources? Show how you work this out.

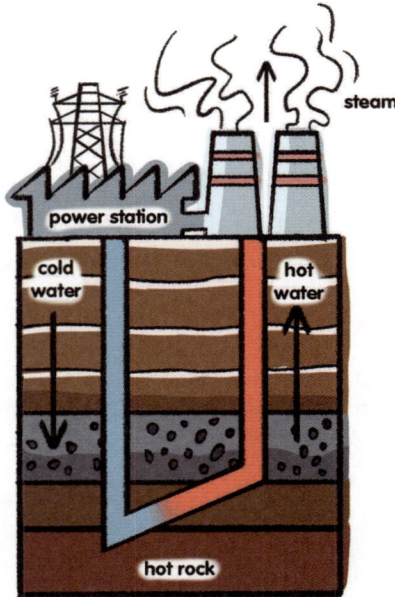

steam

power station

cold water

hot water

hot rock

**b**

One cubic kilometre (1 km³) of rock at 2500 °C contains as much stored energy as 40 million barrels of oil.

During a 2010 volcanic eruption in Iceland, 1.3 km³ of lava flowed out of the volcano at an average temperature of 1000 °C.

Lava is rock that has melted to liquid form. For this question, assume that 1 km³ of lava contains approximately as much stored energy as 1 km³ of rock.

How can you estimate the energy in the lava as equivalent barrels of oil? Give reasons for your decisions.

_____

_____

**3** Discuss this chart with a partner.

- What do you notice?
- What questions can you ask?
- How can you find the answers to your questions?

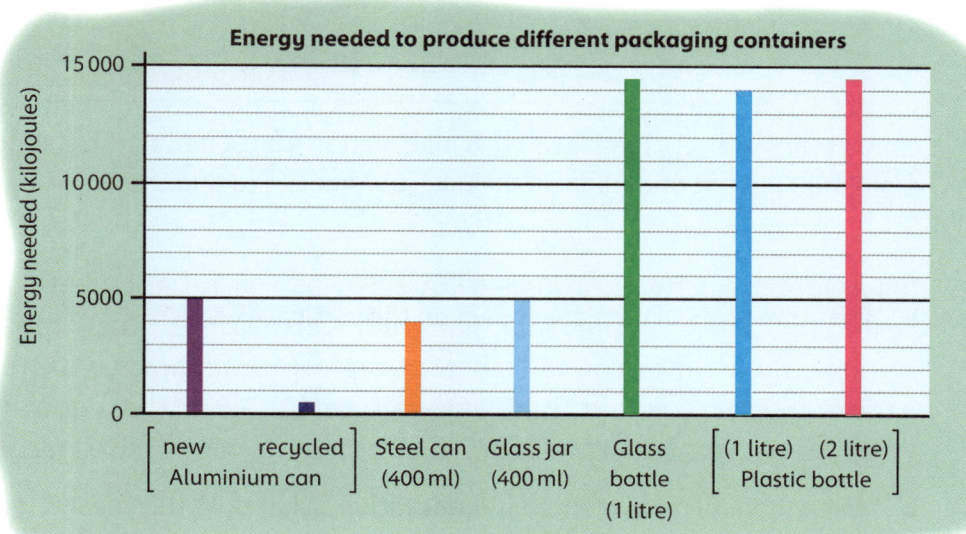

**4** Use information from the graph to answer these questions.

**a** Nadja bought six cans of cola (recycled aluminium), 5 tins of vegetables in steel cans, 1 glass jar of pickles and 1 litre of olive oil in a glass bottle.

What was the total energy needed to produce the containers for these items?

**b** Silvana says that less energy is used to produce a 1-litre plastic bottle than a glass bottle, so we should buy plastic bottles.

Maria says that it is more sustainable to use glass bottles. Explain why Maria might say this.

## Let's solve …

**1** An environmental organization produced this chart.

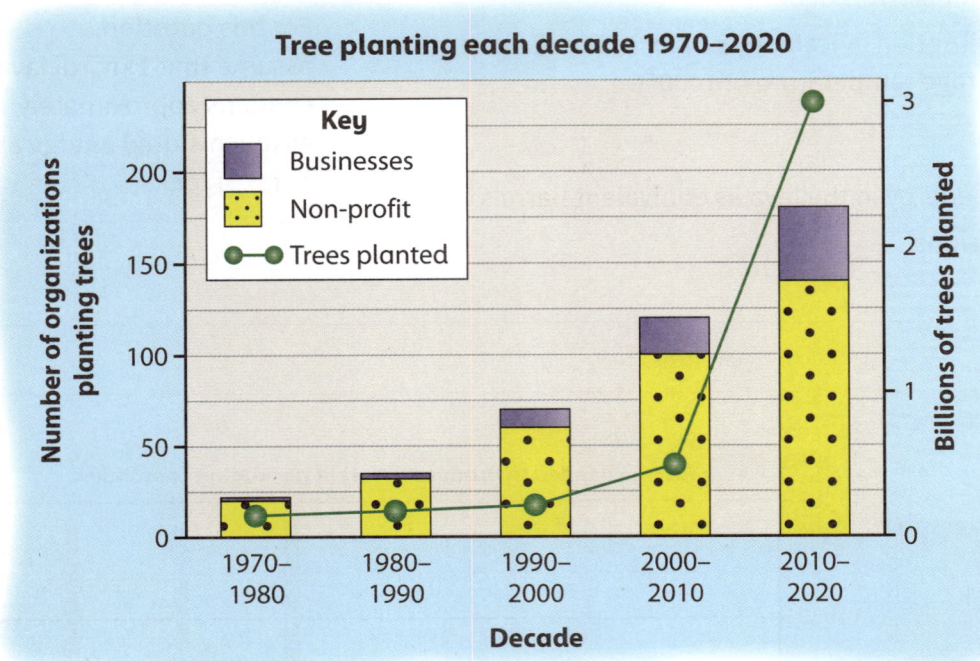

**Tree planting each decade 1970–2020**

Source: Martin, M. P. et al (2021). People plant trees for utility more often than for biodiversity or carbon. *Biological Conservation, 261, 109224.* https://doi.org/10.1016/j.biocon.2021.109224

**a** What three sets of data are shown on the vertical axes?

_____          _____

_____

**b** The number of trees planted is **cumulative**. What does this mean?

_____

**c** Has the ratio of non-profit organizations to business organizations changed much over 5 decades? Support your answer mathematically.

_____

**2** For each question, write a number sentence to show how you would solve it. Then use a calculator to work out the solution.

**a** Approximately how many trees were planted between 2010 and 2020?

_____

**b** For the decade 2010–2020, 18% of organizations monitored the trees after planting. Estimate how many organizations did not monitor the trees.

_____

**c** Only 5% of the organizations who planted trees between 2010 and 2020 measured the survival rates of trees. How many organizations is this?

_____

**3** Dora Sanchez used to be a cattle farmer in Colombia. In 2012, she started planting trees on her 56-hectare (ha) ranch. By 2023, she had restored 40 ha of jungle and now she runs the La Ñupana Nature Reserve.

A hectare is equivalent to the area of a square with 100 m sides.

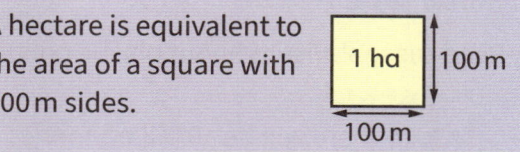

**a** Calculate the area of the jungle in La Ñupana in square metres (m²).

**b** How many hectares of trees did Dora plant per year on average to cover an area of 40 ha?

_____

_____

**4** In 2020, a large pharmaceutical company pledged to plant and maintain 50 million trees by the end of 2025.

**a** At the end of June 2023, the company had planted 10.5 million trees. How many more did it need to plant per month to meet the original target?

_____

**b** At the end of June 2023, the company changed the target to 200 million trees by the end of 2030. How many trees does it need to plant in each 6-month period to meet this goal?

**5** The company is going to plant four types of trees. The table gives information about the probability of picking each type of tree at random.

| Type of tree | Kapok | Rubber | Teak | Balsa |
|---|---|---|---|---|
| Probability | 0.25 | $y$ | 0.35 | $3y$ |

If you pick a tree at random, calculate the probability it will be a rubber tree.

_____

_____

### Read, talk, reason

1  Read these statistics about plastic pollution.

- By 2025 there will be 10 billion tonnes of plastic waste on Earth.

- One million plastic bottles are bought every minute. 85% of them are not recycled.

- About 8 000 000 tonnes of plastic end up in the oceans each year.

- The World Economic Forum (WEF) estimates that by 2050 there will be 850 million tonnes of plastic in the oceans and 812 million tonnes of fish.

- In 2018, 482 billion plastic bottles were used. This number rose to 600 billion in 2021.

Discuss these questions in groups.

a  Which statistic is the most shocking to you? Why?

b  In 2021 the world population was 7 900 000 000. How does that compare with the number of plastic bottles used that year?

c  By 2025, there will be around 8.2 billion people on Earth. Predict how much plastic waste there will be per person in 2025.

d  Why do you think the number of plastic bottles used each year is increasing so much?

e  Why is plastic pollution everyone's problem?

2  Flip flops are the world's most popular shoe. Three billion pairs of flip flops are sold each year.

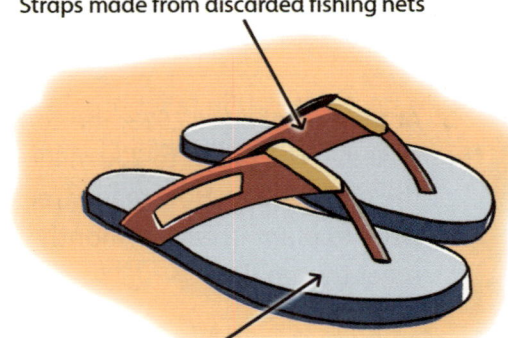

Straps made from discarded fishing nets

Soles made from recycled ocean waste

a  Look at these flip flops. How can they make a difference to ocean pollution levels? Give two reasons.

_____

_____

One pair of these flip flops is made from approximately 1 kg of plastic ocean waste, including about 24 single-use plastic bottles.

b  How many tonnes of plastic waste would be removed from the oceans if $\frac{1}{4}$ of all flip flops sold in a year were made from recycled materials?

_____

c  How many plastic bottles would be recycled to make these flip flops?

_____

**3** At a UN conference on sustainability in 2015, a sportswear company teamed up with a global environmental organization. They work together to reduce plastic ocean waste.

One of their first products was a running shoe containing 75% marine plastic waste. Each pair of shoes contains the equivalent of 11 single-use plastic bottles.

**a** In 2017, the company sold 1 million pairs of these running shoes. The next year they sold 5 times as many. In 2019, they sold 11 million pairs and in 2020, their sales increased by another 4 million pairs. Draw a simple mathematical model to show the growth in sales over time.

**b** The average mass of one single-use plastic bottle is 30 g. What is the mass of single-use plastic bottles used to make each shoe?

_____

_____

**4** The partnership sponsors an annual event called *Run for the Oceans*. Participants in the event use a special app to track their running. The partnership pledges that for every 10 minutes of running tracked, they will remove 1 bottle from the ocean (up to a maximum mass of 250 000 kg).

**a** In 2017, 60 000 runners took part in the event. In 2020, 6.7 million runners took part. How much bigger was the 2020 event than the 2017 event?

_____

_____

**b** How many minutes of running do participants need to track to remove the maximum mass of 250 000 kg from the oceans? Show your working.

## Let's reason …

**1** Conservationists in North America (USA and Canada) produced this chart. It shows the percentage of bird species at each level of conservation concern.

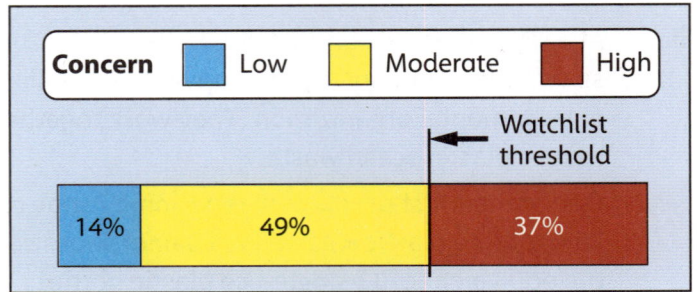

**a** There are 1154 species of birds in North America. How many species are on the watchlist?

_____

**b** Is it correct to say that one-third of the bird species in North America need urgent conservation action? Give a reason for your answer.

_____

**c** Volunteers at a bird protection charity each pick a bird species at random to monitor. What is the probability of picking a species that is not on the conservation watchlist?

This is how Lydia and Owain worked this out.

Lydia
$$\frac{14}{100} + \frac{49}{100} = \frac{63}{100} = 0.63$$

Owain
$$1 - 0.37 = 0.63$$

Explain in your own words what each student did to work out the probability.

Lydia _____

_____

Owain _____

_____

**2** This chart shows similar information to the North American chart, but for a different region of the world.

Discuss these questions in groups.

**a** How are the charts similar? How do they differ?

**b** What do you need to do to redraw this chart in the same format as the North American chart?

**c** What additional information do you need to draw a chart like this one for the North American birds?

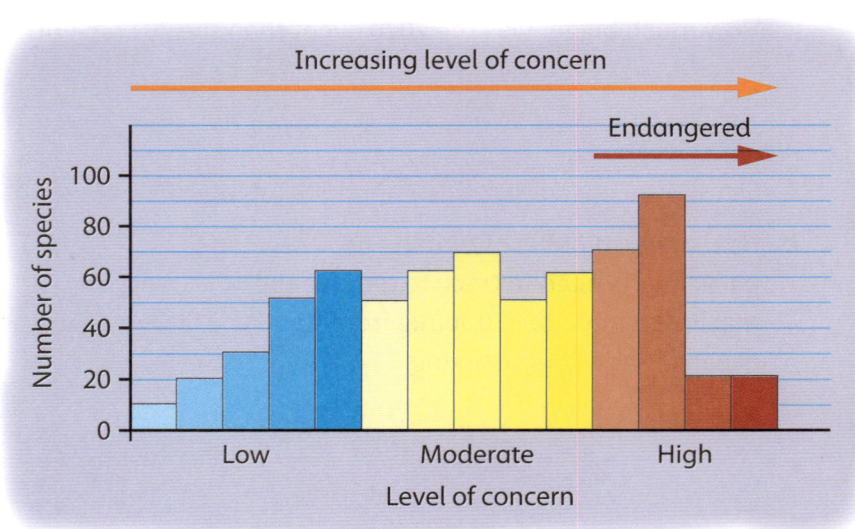

**3** Thanks to conservation action, the population of an endangered species of bird is increasing at a rate of 5% per year. The current population is 380 birds.

**a** Sal is working out how many birds there will be in 5 years' time if the population continues to grow at this rate. Here is his working:

> *5 years at 5% = 25%   25% of 380 = 95*
> *380 + 95 = 475 birds*

What has Sal done wrong?

_____

**b** Now work out the number of birds in 5 years' time. Show how you work it out.

**c** Draw a mathematical model to show how the bird population will increase over the next 20 years at this rate.

**d** Use your model to predict how many years it will take for the population to reach 1000 birds.

_____ years

**e** Why are your answers only predictions and not certain amounts? Give one reason.

_____

## Think, talk, write

**1** Suki read the 2022 *State of the Rhino* report published by the International Rhino Foundation. She made these summary notes.

**a** Discuss her notes with your partner.

- What do you notice?
- What do you wonder?

White rhino
2012 peak – 21 320
2021 – 15 942

Total world
population
2007 – 24 615
2012 peak – 29 646
2021 – 29 266

Black rhino
1995 – 2300
2017 – 5496
2021 – 6195

In 1973, only 3512 white rhinos left in the world

South Africa has 50% of the world's black rhinos and 12 968 white rhinos.

**b** Suki started to graph the data, but she did not finish drawing or labelling her graph.

Work with your partner. Use the information that Suki collected to finish the graph and the key.

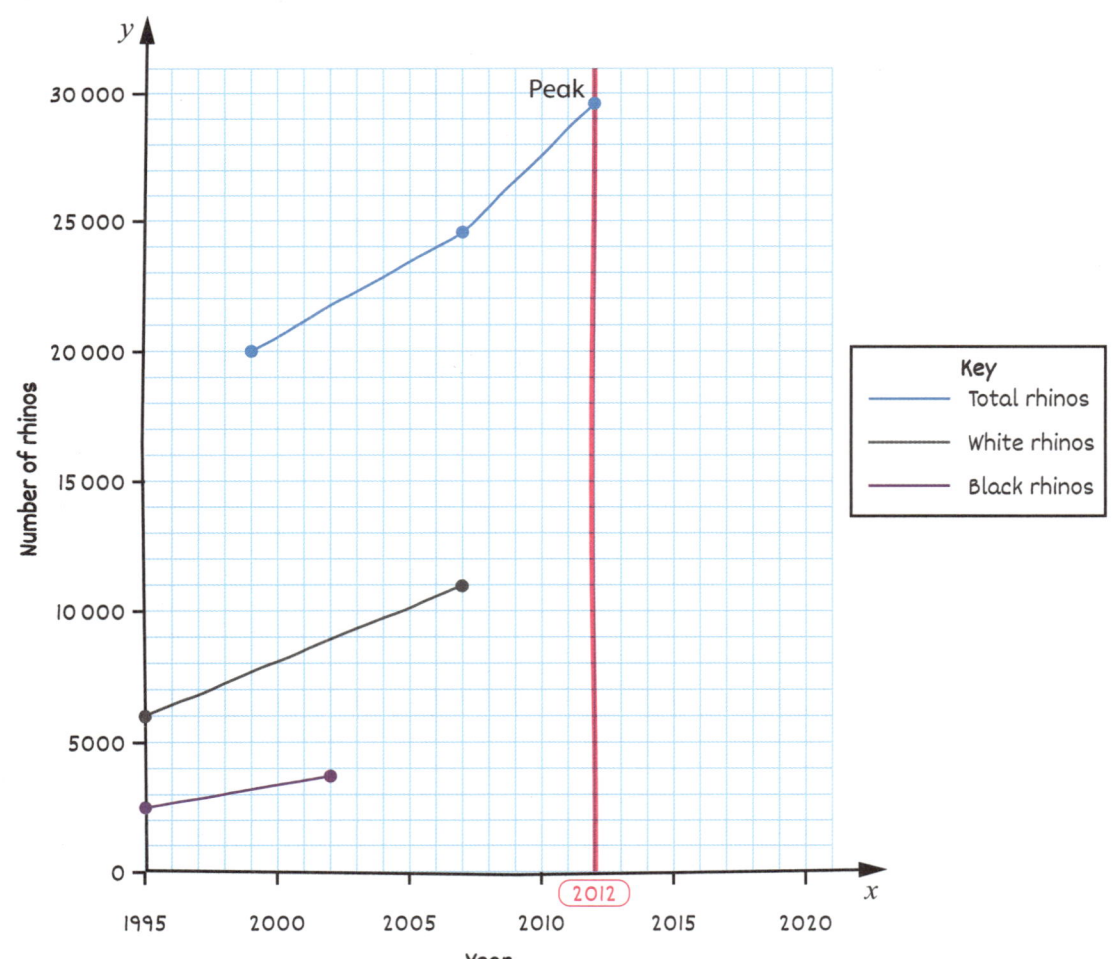

**2** Study this graph from the 2022 *State of the Rhino* report. Use the data to answer the questions.

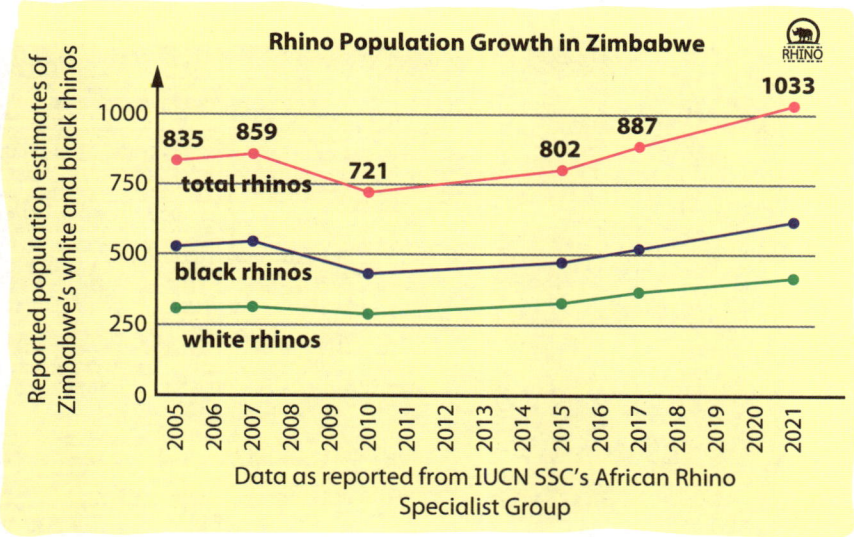

**a** What is the overall trend in rhino numbers shown on this graph?

_____

**b** How is this trend different from the trend shown on the graph for the whole world?

_____

**c** If you drew a graph like this for South Africa, what differences would there be? List at least two.

_____

_____

**d** Describe how black rhino numbers in Zimbabwe changed between 2007 and 2010.

_____

**e** What happened to white rhino numbers in Zimbabwe in the same period?

_____

**f** During which period did the number of black and white rhinos in Zimbabwe increase at the same rate? How do you know this?

_____

**g** What percentage of the world's rhino population was in Zimbabwe in 2021? Show how you calculate this.

_____

→ Turn back to page 4 and complete the problem-solving record.

### Think, talk, write

1 Work in pairs.

Look at this photograph of trains parked outside a station.

- What do you notice?
- What do you wonder?
- What maths can you see?

2 Some trains are very long. Read this information from a news article about a record-length train. Highlight or underline all the measurements and quantities.

This weekend, a freight train 5.6 km long was tested in Southern California. The train was almost three times the length of a typical 1.6 km freight train. It had 295 rail cars, carrying more than 600 cargo containers, mostly double-stacked. Nine locomotives (engines) were spread along the train.

The train was the longest that the rail company had ever assembled. Because of its great length, it was not allowed to travel at more than 105 km/h. It took 3 to 5 minutes to cross a railway crossing, resulting in longer waiting times for motorists at the crossing.

The engineer said that the longer waiting time for motorists was actually an advantage. She explained that the long train was the equivalent of 3 trains of normal length. Because the signals begin stopping traffic 20 to 25 seconds before each train arrives, the total of the waiting times for 3 normal-length trains to cross would be 40 to 50 seconds longer.

Traffic officials are worried about the length of time needed to safely stop a train that is over 5 km long, as well as possible delays for emergency services if crossings are blocked for longer than 5 minutes.

a In the USA, the maximum length of freight trains is 3658 m because of the time it takes for a long train to stop. How much longer is the freight train described in the article?

_____

_____

**b** In Europe, most freight trains are 740 m long. Find two ways of comparing this length mathematically with the train in the article.

_____

_____

**3** Trains cannot swerve or stop quickly. The train driver has to apply the brake and wait for the train to stop. The table gives information about different freight trains.

| Train mass and length | Stopping time (seconds) | Stopping distance (metres) |
|---|---|---|
| 8400 tonnes, 1500 m | 90 | 2155 |
| 2020 tonnes, 1500 m | 58 | 1400 |
| 2750 tonnes, 1280 m | 75 | 1860 |
| 3450 tonnes, 1600 m | 82 | 2025 |

Answer these questions with a partner.

**a** How does the mass of the train affect its stopping time and distance?

_____

**b** Which train took the longest time to stop? _____

**c** Which train stopped in the shortest distance? _____

**d** A passenger train takes about 43 seconds and 180 m to stop. How does that compare with the lightest freight train? Suggest why passenger trains can stop faster than freight trains.

_____

_____

**4** The mass of a freight train depends on the mass of the goods that it is carrying. Work out the mass of the goods on each of these rail cars.

The mass of an empty container is called the **tare weight**.

**a**

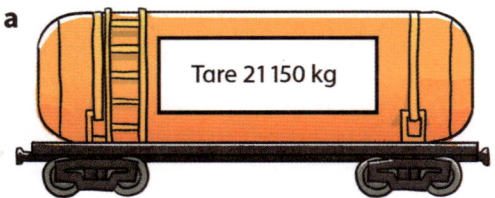

Tare 21 150 kg

fully loaded 116 tonnes

**b**

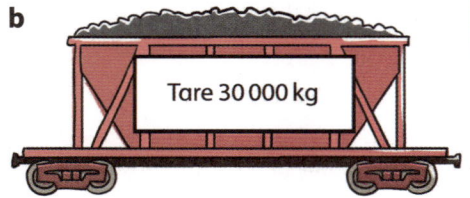

Tare 30 000 kg

fully loaded 96.2 tonnes

_____     _____

### Let's reason ...

Sometimes rail cars need to be moved into a different order in the train. To do this, an engine moves them onto different parts of the track.

The engine and rail cars can be connected and disconnected at the front or the back as needed.

The engine can move rail cars into the sidings (side tracks) to help place them into order.

The engine can move forwards and backwards, so it can push or pull the rail cars (singly or in groups).

 **1** On these diagrams, the block with the arrow represents an engine and the blocks labelled X and Y represent two rail cars.

   **a** Discuss with your partner what each diagram shows.

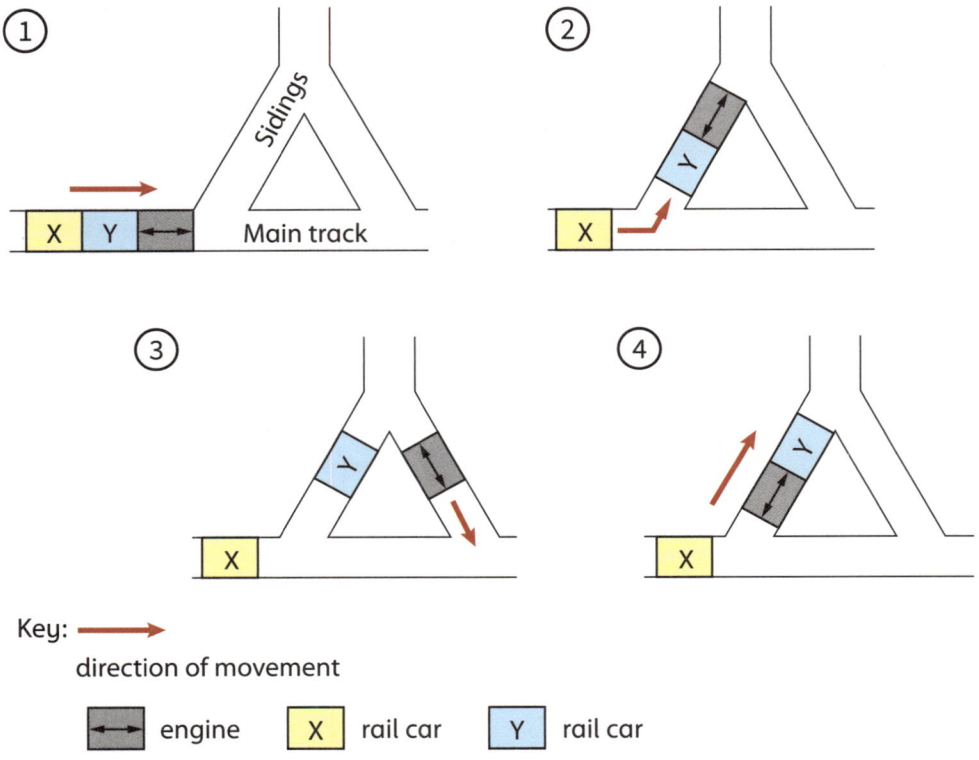

Key: ——→
    direction of movement

     engine    X rail car    Y rail car

   **b** After the engine has finished moving the two rail cars, they are in the positions shown in this diagram. Describe to your partner how the engine driver did this.

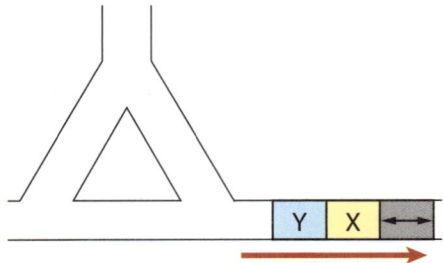

**2** Four engines (A, B, C and D) are parked in the rail yard. They need to move to the other rail line and park in the order shown to be ready for the next day.

How can they do this in the least number of moves?

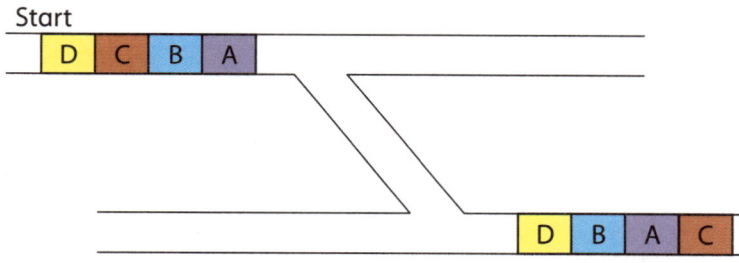

Remember, engines can move forward and backward by themselves.

**3** Work with a partner to find the most efficient way to move these rail cars to make the train shown on the right. You can leave the cars marked X in any siding.

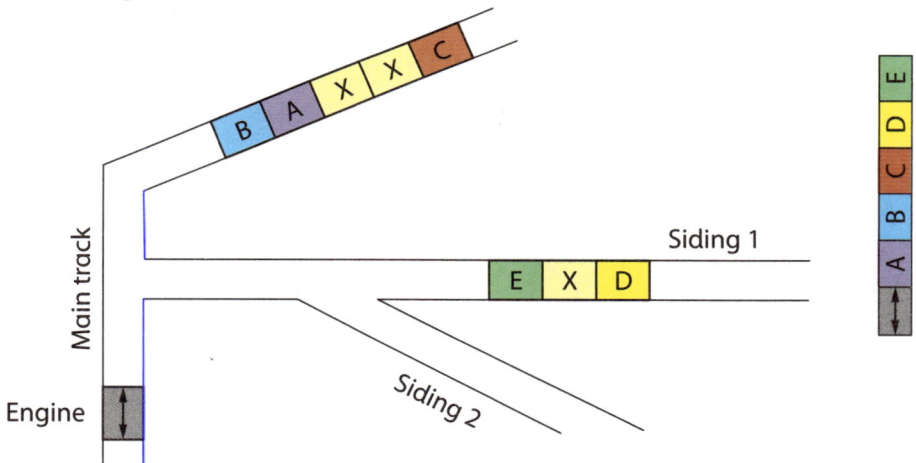

The engine can push or pull and rail cars can be connected and disconnected from each other.

## Think, talk, solve

**1** Study the chart and answer the questions with your partner.

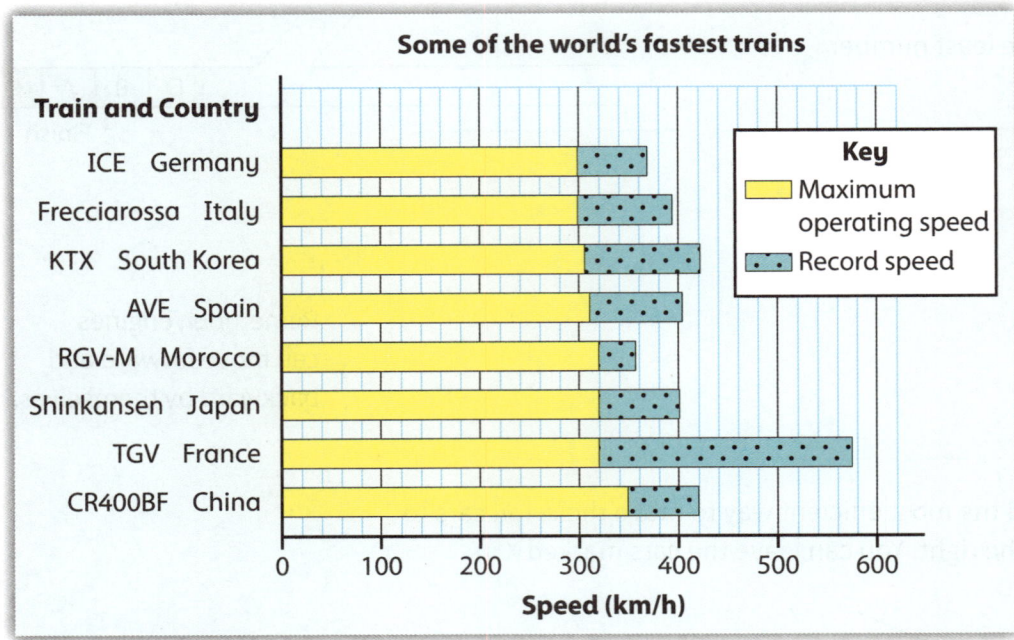

The operating speed is the speed at which the train normally travels.

**a** What does the chart show?

_____

**b** What is the mathematical name for a measurement such as 299 km/h? _____

**c** Which train operates at the highest speed? _____

**d** Which train holds the record for the highest speed? _____

**e** What is the difference between the highest and lowest operating speeds of these trains?

_____

**f** How much faster does the TGV generally travel than the ICE?

_____

**2** Speed, distance and time are related quantities.

Speed = Distance travelled ÷ Time taken

We write $S = \frac{D}{T}$

Use the speed–distance–time triangle to help you write a formula for distance and time.

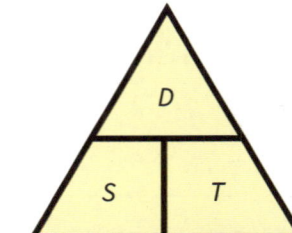

Distance = _____

Time = _____

**3** The table shows the distance and journey times for some train routes in Morocco.

| Route | Marrakech to Rabat | Tangier to Fes | Tangier to Kenitra |
|---|---|---|---|
| Distance (km) | 334 | 306 | 194 |
| Time | 3.5 hours | 4.5 hours | 50 min |
| Average speed | | | |

a Calculate the average speed of each train and complete the table.

b Which route has the fastest train? _____

 **4** The distance by train between Paris (France) and Barcelona (Spain) is 1073 km.

a The TGV from Paris to Barcelona takes 6 hours and 15 min. What is its average speed on that route?

> Remember, time is not a decimal measurement. For example, 0.5 hours means 30 minutes.

 b The AVE from Barcelona to Paris travels at an average speed of 158.18 km/h. How long does that journey take?

 **5** A train travels at a steady speed of 120 km/h for 48 min (0.8 h). What distance does it travel in that time?

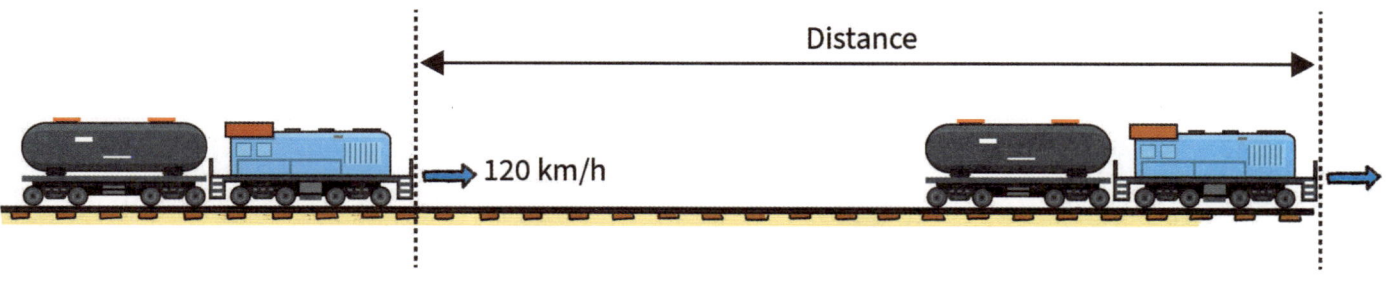

Distance

120 km/h

## Let's reason …

**1** Work in pairs. Ask each other questions to make sure you can read and understand these metro timetables.

| Ali Town | Thokar Niaz Baig | Canal View | Hanjarwal | Wahdat Road | Awan Town | Sabzazar | Shahnoor | |
|---|---|---|---|---|---|---|---|---|
| 06:27 | 06:29 | 06:31 | 06:33 | 06:35 | 06:36 | 06:43 | 06:48 | |
| 06:41 | .. | .. | .. | .. | .. | .. | 06:58 | Express |
| 06:44 | 06:46 | 06:48 | 06:50 | 06:51 | 06:53 | 07:00 | 07:05 | |
| 07:08 | .. | .. | .. | .. | .. | .. | 07:27 | Express |
| 07:25 | 07:27 | 07:29 | 07:32 | 07:33 | 07:35 | 07:42 | 07:48 | |
| 07:33 | .. | .. | .. | .. | .. | .. | 07:52 | Express |
| 07:41 | 07:43 | 07:45 | 07:48 | 07:49 | 07:51 | 07:58 | 08:04 | |
| 07:51 | .. | .. | .. | .. | .. | .. | 08:08 | Express |
| 07:54 | 07:56 | 07:58 | 08:01 | 08:02 | 08:04 | 08:11 | 08:17 | |
| 08:16 | .. | .. | .. | .. | .. | .. | 08:33 | Express |
| 08:20 | 08:22 | 08:24 | 08:27 | 08:28 | 08:30 | 08:37 | 08:43 | |
| 08:34 | .. | .. | .. | .. | .. | .. | 08:51 | Express |
| 08:37 | 08:39 | 08:41 | 08:44 | 08:45 | 08:47 | 08:54 | 09:00 | |
| 08:50 | 08:52 | .. | 08:56 | .. | 08:59 | .. | 09:00 | |
| 09:14 | .. | 09:18 | .. | 09:22 | .. | 09:25 | 09:35 | |
| 09:34 | 09:36 | 09:38 | 09:40 | 09:42 | .. | .. | 09:55 | |

| Shahnoor | Sabzazar | Awan Town | Wahdat Road | Hanjarwal | Canal View | Thokar Niaz Baig | Ali Town |
|---|---|---|---|---|---|---|---|
| 16:05 | 16:09 | 16:17 | 16:19 | 16:20 | 16:22 | 16:24 | 16:28 |
| 16:20 | 16:24 | 16:32 | 16:33 | 16:35 | 16:37 | 16:39 | 16:43 |
| 16:36 | .. | .. | .. | .. | .. | .. | 16:54 |
| 16:39 | 16:43 | 16:52 | 16:54 | 16:56 | 16:58 | 17:00 | 17:04 |
| 16:47 | .. | .. | .. | .. | .. | .. | 17:05 |
| 17:02 | .. | .. | .. | .. | .. | .. | 17:20 |
| 17:04 | 17:08 | 17:15 | 17:17 | 17:19 | 17:21 | 17:23 | 17:27 |
| 17:14 | .. | .. | .. | .. | .. | .. | 17:31 |
| 17:19 | .. | .. | .. | .. | .. | .. | 17:37 |
| 17:23 | 17:27 | 17:35 | 17:37 | 17:39 | 17:41 | 17:43 | 17:46 |

**2** Amira uses the Orange Metro train to travel from home to college. She catches the train at Ali Town and gets off at Shahnoor. She walks for 15 minutes from Shahnoor station to the college.

  **a** On Monday and Wednesday, Amira needs to be at college by 8:15 a.m. She catches the latest possible train. Which train is this?

  _____

  **b** On Tuesday and Thursday, Amira starts college later, at 10 a.m. What is the latest train she can catch at Ali Town?

  _____

  **c** Amira goes to the library every day after college to study. She must be back at Ali Town by half past five so her brother can drive her home. What is the latest train she can catch?

  _____

**3** Nafiz attends the same college and has the same class times. He catches the train at Canal View.

  **a** Why can't Nafiz catch the same train as Amira on Monday and Wednesday?

  _____

  **b** Nafiz needs to be at Canal View station by 5 p.m. on Monday. What time should he leave college to catch the latest possible train?

  _____

**4** A train leaves Pasar Seni station every 9 minutes. A bus leaves from the station every 15 minutes. A train and a bus both leave the station at 6:30 a.m. What is the next time that a train and a bus leave the station at the same time?

**5** Trains A, B and C all leave Fort Station on Friday morning to travel to Walpola.

Train A leaves 15 minutes after Train B and arrives at Walpola 15 minutes before it.

Train B takes 52 minutes to get to Walpola and arrives at 11:30.

Train C leaves 25 minutes before Train B and arrives 20 minutes after Train A.

Work out what time each train left Fort Station.

In Europe, you can buy a train pass that allows you to travel on national train lines in 33 countries. The costs of different types of pass are shown in the table.

**1** Discuss the table with a partner.
- What do you notice?
- What do you wonder?

### Cost in euros (€) of different types of European train passes

| Pass type | Valid for ... | Youth (under 28) | Adult (28–59) | Senior (over 60) |
|---|---|---|---|---|
| **Flexible** (any days during the time period) | 4 days in 1 month | 194 | 258 | 232 |
| | 5 days in 1 month | 223 | 296 | 267 |
| | 7 days in 1 month | 264 | 352 | 317 |
| | 10 days in 2 months | 316 | 421 | 375 |
| | 15 days in 2 months | 389 | 518 | 466 |
| **Consecutive** | 15 days | 349 | 465 | 419 |
| | 22 days | 408 | 544 | 489 |
| | 1 month | 528 | 704 | 633 |
| | 2 months | 575 | 768 | 691 |
| | 3 months | 711 | 947 | 853 |

 **2** Ani, a 19-year-old, is going to Europe for 3 weeks. She will arrive and depart from Italy. She also plans to visit France, Switzerland and Slovenia.

**a** Ani only plans to use the train to travel between countries. Which is the cheapest pass for her to buy? Why?

_____

**b** How much cheaper is this pass than the adult pass of the same type?

_____

**3** Mason wants to buy **consecutive** 15-day passes for three people aged 29, 33 and 70.

**a** What will the total cost for the three passes be?

_____

**b** Mason finds the prices of single train tickets for the route they plan to travel. There are four train journeys on the route, and the cheapest tickets are €193, €78, €41 and €70 per person. What will it cost to buy three lots of the single tickets instead of the three passes?

_____

**c** What is the difference in price between the three passes and the three lots of single tickets?

_____

**4** A travel agent books consecutive 1-month youth passes for 10 young people.
He gets a 15% discount on the price. What is the total cost?

_____

**5** A travel agent books flexible 15 days in 2 months passes for a family of 3 youths,
4 adults and 2 seniors. She charges a booking fee of 2.5% of the total cost.
What price will the family pay?

_____

**6** These two graphs compare the cost of travelling by train and plane on two different routes.

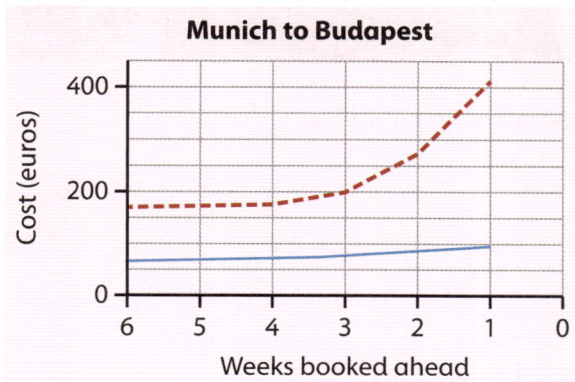 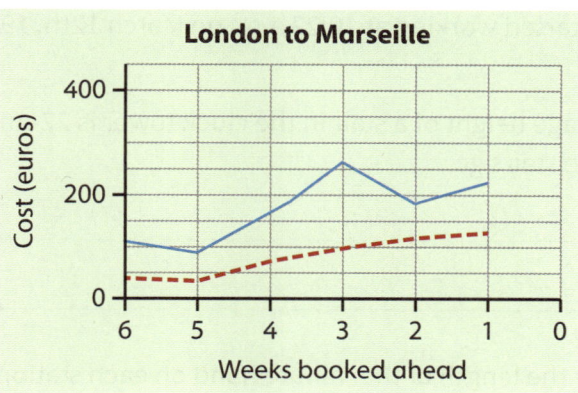 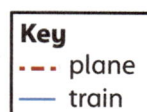

Fill in the missing words and numbers in these sentences.

**a** It is cheaper to travel by _____ than by _____ from
Munich to Budapest.

**b** It is more expensive to travel by _____ than by _____
from London to Marseille.

**c** On all routes it is _____ to book 6 weeks before you travel.

**d** It costs € _____ to book a flight from Munich to Budapest 1 week before

you travel. The same trip by train costs € _____.

**e** You have to buy the most expensive train ticket from London to Marseille if you

book _____ weeks before travel and the ticket will cost € _____.

**f** If you book a flight 6 weeks before you travel from London to Marseille, it only costs

€ _____. This is € _____ cheaper than travelling by train.

**g** If you book 1 week before you travel from Munich to Budapest you can save € _____ by

booking a _____ ticket rather than a _____ ticket.

## Think, talk, solve

**1** Read the information about the largest train station in Australia.

Sydney's Central Railway Station opened in 1906. It is the busiest station in Australia and is one of the biggest railway stations in the world. Approximately 86 million passengers use the station each year.

The station's clock tower is one of the tallest in the world. It is 75 metres high, each of the four round clock faces is 4.7 metres in diameter and there are 302 stairs to the top. The clocks started working at 10:22 a.m. on March 12th, 1921.

**a** The average height of a stair in the clock tower is 22 cm. Estimate how far up the tower the stairs go.

_____

_____

**b** Estimate the length of the minute hand on each station clock. Explain how you got your answer.

_____

_____

**c** What is the average number of passengers using the station per week?

_____

**d** Estimate how long the station clocks have been working in years, months and weeks. Show how you get your answer.

**e** In 2023, the population of Sydney was approximately 5.28 million. How many times greater than that is the number of passengers using the station each year?

_____

_____

**2** Japan has the busiest train stations in the world.

| Station | Passengers per day (millions) | Number of rail lines |
|---|---|---|
| Shinjuku | 3.59 | 11 |
| Ikebukuro | 2.62 | 8 |
| Umeda | 2.40 | 12 |
| Shibuya | 2.30 | 8 |
| Yokohama | 2.24 | 10 |

**a** The passenger numbers in the table are rounded estimates. Tell your partner how you know this.

**b** Yuki says:

> Shibuya and Yokohama Stations are busier than Umeda Station because they have fewer lines.

What mathematics has Yuki done to work this out?

_____

_____

**c** How many more passengers use Shinjuku Station each year than Yokohama Station? Show two different ways of calculating this.

_____

_____

**3** The diagram shows a turnstile at a platform. The turnstile has three arms, which have equal angles between them. Each time a passenger goes through the turnstile the arms turn 120°.

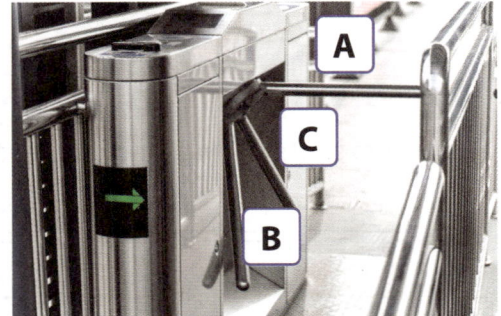

**a** In one hour 26 passengers go through the turnstile. What position will arm A be in after this? Write A, B or C.

[    ]

**b** In one day 438 passengers go through the turnstile. How many times will the turnstile make a complete turn during the day?

[                    ]

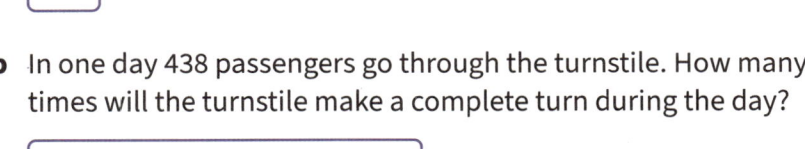

Turn back to page 4 and complete the problem-solving record.

## Think, talk, reason

**1** Since ancient times, people have made up interesting puzzles, riddles and games using mathematics. Discuss these questions with a partner.

- Which of these maths games or puzzles have you heard of or played?

- Which would you be interested to try (or play more of)? Why?

sudoku    KenKen puzzles    maths riddles    logic puzzles

word sums    tangrams    magic squares and triangles

> Are there any that you haven't heard of? For each one, try to guess what kind of game or puzzle it might be. You can also look them up online.

**2** This is a photograph of the Rhind papyrus. It is an artefact from ancient Egypt. The Rhind papyrus contains this riddle:

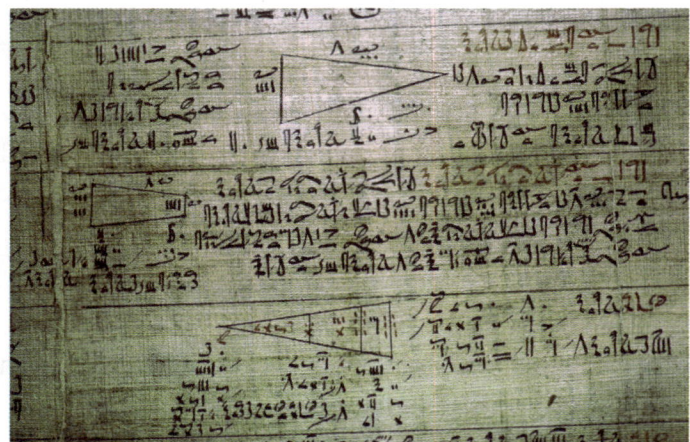

> 7 houses each have 7 cats.
>
> Each cat kills 7 mice.
>
> Each mouse has eaten 7 ears of barley.
>
> Each ear of barley would have grown 7 hekats of barley.
>
> **How many things is this altogether?**

**a** Laura reads the riddle. She wonders whether to use addition or multiplication. What advice would you give her?

_____

_____

> A hekat was a unit of volume. But you don't need to know how much it was to solve the riddle.
>
> The question is asking you to add up all the houses, cats, mice, ears of barley and hekats.

**b** Laura starts solving the riddle by drawing seven houses, like this:

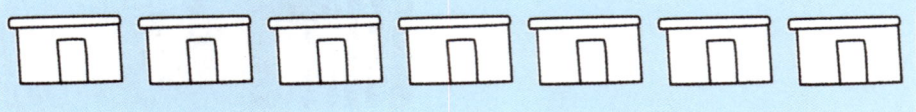

Discuss Laura's strategy with a partner. What problem will she have with this strategy?

_____

**c** With your partner, find a way to calculate the answer.

**d** Laura says she can use this riddle to make any number of new riddles, by replacing the number 7 with the letter $n$. Write the formula she could use to calculate the answer for the new riddle.

_____

**3** Read this information about the Rhind papyrus and other Egyptian artefacts. Use it to solve the problems below.

> The Rhind papyrus was written in Ancient Egypt around 1550 BCE. It was purchased by Alexander Henry Rhind in 1858 CE. An even older artefact, the Akhmim wooden tablet, was written around 2000 BCE. It showed that the Ancient Egyptians used fractions to divide their units of measurement for grains.

**a** How much older is the Akhmim wooden tablet than the Rhind papyrus?

**b** How old was each artefact in 1858 CE when Alexander Rhind purchased the papyrus?

Rhind papyrus _____

Akhmim wooden tablet _____

**c** How old is each artefact this year?

Rhind papyrus _____

Akhmim wooden tablet _____

**d** Use your working from questions **b** and **c**. Write a formula to calculate the age of each artefact in any year.

Use $y$ for the year.

A magic square is an array of numbers in rows and columns. All the numbers in each row, column and diagonal add up to the same sum. The sum is called the 'magic constant'. There are different kinds of magic squares:

Standard magic squares only use positive whole numbers.

In trivial magic squares, some numbers are repeated.

In semi-magic squares, the diagonals do not add up to the magic constant.

## Think, talk, solve

1 The photograph shows a famous magic square from a building in Barcelona, Spain. Which words best describe this square?

a standard and trivial ☐

b trivial and semi-magic ☐

c standard and semi-magic ☐

2 What is the magic constant of the square in the photograph?

3 Discuss the photograph with a partner.
- What do you notice?
- What do you wonder?

**4** This is a simple 3 × 3 magic square. Complete the square so it contains all the numbers 1 to 9.

It is easy to complete, but can you explain your thinking as you go along? Try this: as you calculate each missing number, explain your reasoning, or what you tried and what it showed.

| 4 | | |
|---|---|---|
| 9 | | 1 |
| | 7 | |

_____

_____

_____

_____

_____

**5** In fact, there are only 8 ways to make a 3 × 3 magic square with the numbers 1 to 9. They are all either reflections or rotations of the same pattern. They all have the same magic constant.

Using this information, complete these two magic squares.

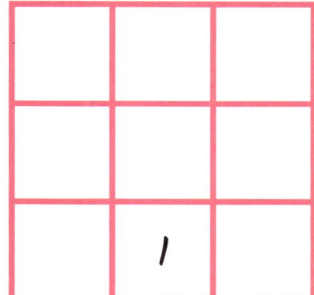

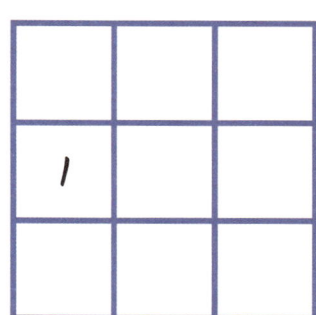

**Let's solve …**

**6** This 4 × 4 magic square uses negative numbers. Work out the missing values. Use the box below for your working.

Each negative number from −5 to −20 must appear once. The magic constant is a multiple of −10.

| −13 | | −7 | −20 |
|---|---|---|---|
| | −19 | | −9 |
| −18 | −5 | | |
| | | −17 | |

### Think, talk, solve

This type of puzzle is traditionally called a matchstick puzzle, but you can use any short sticks – toothpicks, ice cream sticks, pencils or even strips of cardboard.

1  Dineo arranged 15 ice cream sticks to form 5 squares of the same size, like this. She gave her friends this challenge:
   'Take away 3 sticks and leave 3 squares.'

**Ali**

> I moved 3 sticks and made 4 squares.

**Bo**

> I took away 3 sticks but I made an L-shape and a rectangle.

**Cam**

> I did it! The answer makes a symmetrical pattern.

Discuss the puzzle with a partner.

a  Ali and Bo didn't solve the puzzle, but each of them made different shapes. Can you do what they did?

b  Can you follow Cam's advice to solve Dineo's puzzle?

> You can draw your solution, or make it using sticks, strips of card or paper, or other materials.

2  Dineo calls the next puzzle 'the magic trick'.
   Sketch or show your solution in the box.

> Move 3 sticks to turn the vase into a cube.

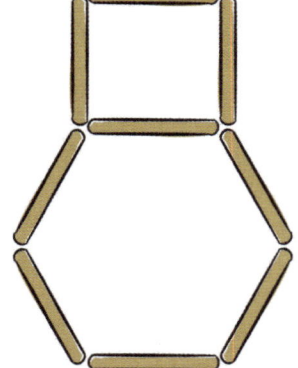

> Sketch a cube from a few different angles. What do you notice about squares and hexagons in your sketches?

**3** For Dineo's next puzzle, she arranged 20 sticks to make 4 squares: 2 small and 2 large. This puzzle also has two different answers.

*Move 4 sticks to make 3 shapes that are all exactly the same size and shape.*

The easy way is to make three squares. The tricky way is to make three 6-sided shapes.

Work with a partner to find the solution. Show or explain your solution here.

**4** Create your own stick puzzle for a friend to solve using squares or triangles.

## Think, talk, solve

**1** Discuss this puzzle with a partner.

Write the numbers 1 to 5 in the circles so that the three numbers on any line add up to 9.

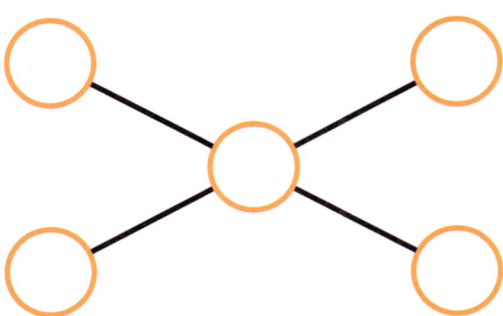

Use the box on page 49 for any of your working out in this lesson.

**2** Write the numbers 1 to 7 in the circles so that the three numbers on any line add up to 12.

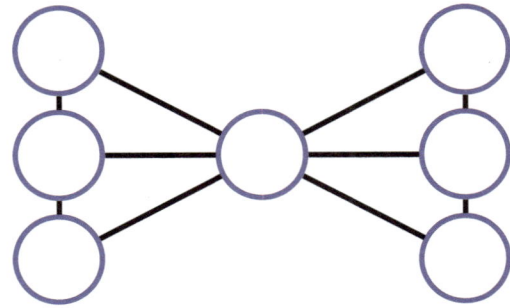

Cut out pieces of paper and write the numbers on them. Try some different arrangements.

Start by working out which numbers cannot share a line.

**3** The smallest size of magic triangle has three numbers along each side and uses the numbers 1 to 6. Work with a partner to make four different magic triangles. Arrange the numbers 1 to 6 in the circles so that all the sides sum to the number given.

**a**

9

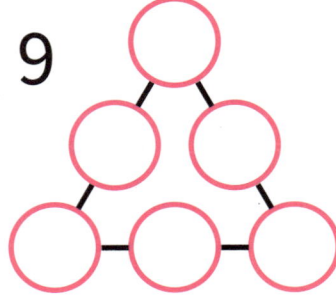

**c**

11

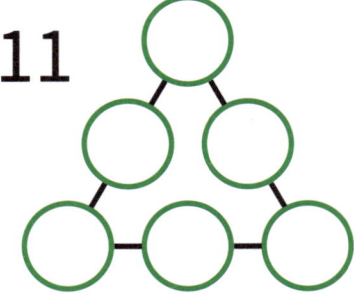

**b**

10

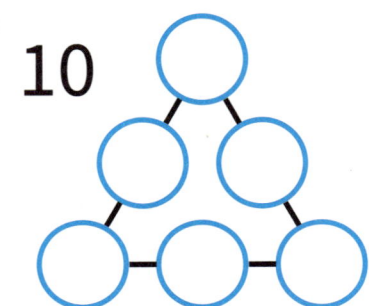

**d**

12

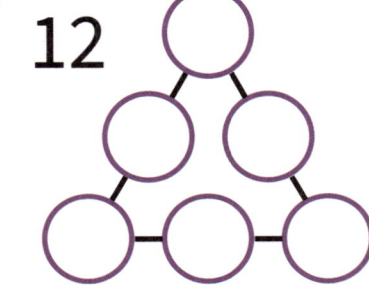

## Let's solve ...

The triangles you solved in question 3 are called 'order 3' triangles, because each side sum has 3 numbers. The frames on this page are for order 4 triangles. There are 18 different ways to solve these triangles.

**4** Choose <u>one</u> of these magic constants (side sum totals): 17, 19, 20, 21, 23.
Find <u>two</u> different ways to complete the triangles using the numbers 1 to 9.

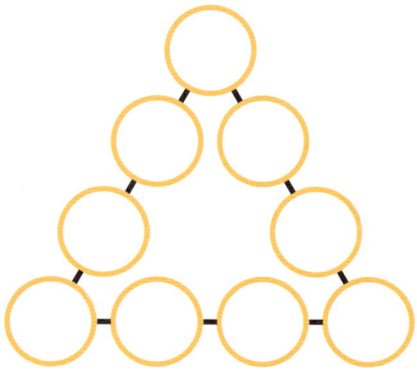 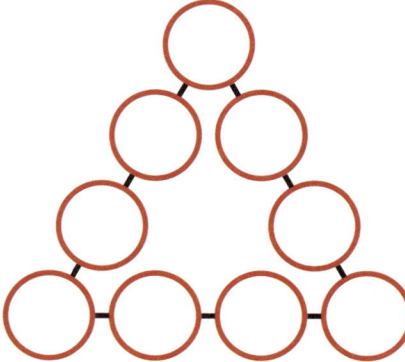

**5 a** Tell a partner the magic constant you chose, and give them two clues for numbers at the vertices. Ask your partner to try to work out your exact triangles.

**b** Solve your partner's magic triangles.

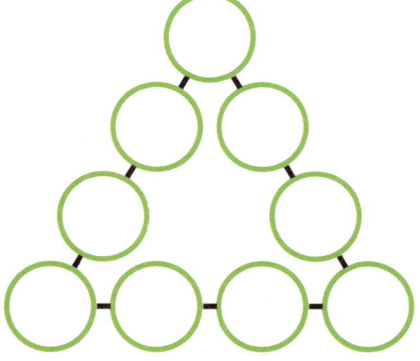 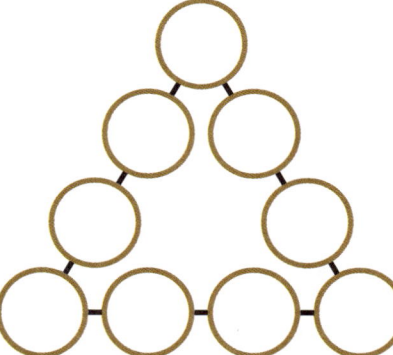

### Think, talk, reason

The tangram is an ancient **rearrangement** game. It dates back to the third century CE, when a Chinese mathematician called Liu Hui rearranged parts of a square to prove some important rules about squares and triangles.

**1** Look at the shapes of the tangram. Discuss it with a partner.

- What shapes do you see?

- What angles do you notice?

- Talk about two different ways you could sort the tangram shapes.

**2** Together the two large triangles make up half of the shape. Express the tangram shape as the sum of seven fractions. Each fraction represents the area taken up by one of the shapes.

_____

**3** In the third century, Liu Hui did an experiment. He cut up a square into these shapes.    He rearranged the four triangles like this.

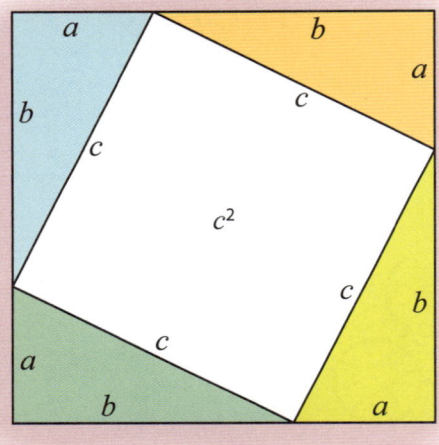 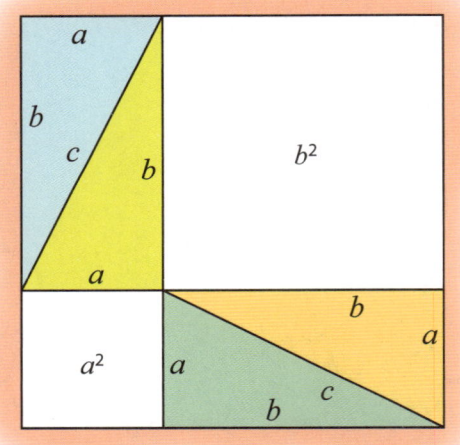

Try Liu Hui's experiment for yourself. Follow the instructions and fill in the gaps.

**a** • On the grid on page 51, draw a square using these lengths:

  $a = 3\,cm$ and $b = 4\,cm$

  Each side of the square is _____ cm long.

- Label each side of the smaller square inside the big square with the letter $c$.

  $c =$ _____ cm

**b** • Draw another square the same size as the first.

- Draw the lines to show the rearrangement of the four triangles.

- Calculate the area of each rectangle and square.

To play the tangram game, players get a silhouette (a completely black shape). They try to make the exact shape using all seven tangram pieces. The pieces must not overlap.

If you don't have a tangram set, use card to cut out your own. Then try to arrange the pieces to make these shapes.

4  Try these tangram puzzles – they are all buildings.

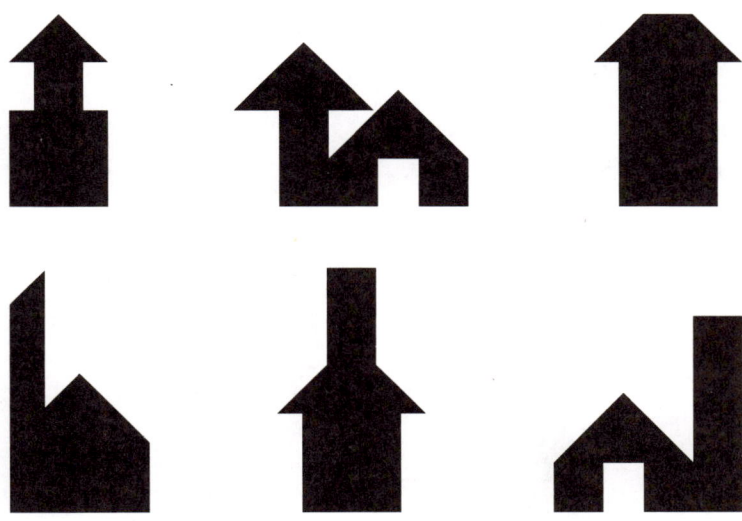

5  You already know that the seven tangram pieces make a square. It is also possible to rearrange the seven tangram pieces to make this shape. It looks the same as the square, but it has a space in the middle.

a  Try to make this shape with your tangram pieces.

b  Discuss with a partner how it is possible that the tangram pieces seem to make the same shape but with an area missing!

## Think, talk, reason

When you use algebra, you use letters or symbols to represent a value in an **equation**. Some puzzles use pictures instead of letters. Each picture represents a value.

**1 a** Here is an easy picture puzzle. You can work it out in one step.

**b** There are a lot of different strategies you can use. Tick the one you used. Discuss the other strategies with a partner. How could you use each strategy to solve the puzzle?

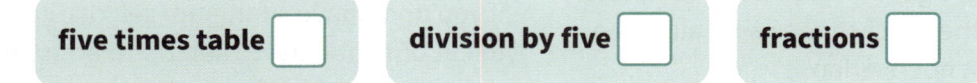

**2** More complicated picture puzzles have more than one equation. You need to look at them all and identify which equation you can solve first. Work with a partner to answer these questions.

- Which equation can you solve first?
- When you have solved the first equation, what information does it give you to solve the next equation?

> It is always easiest to solve the equation that uses the same picture.

**3** Sometimes all of the equations use more than one picture. Discuss with a partner how you can solve this puzzle.

> Which fruit represents the greater number? How much greater is it than the other number? Can you use trial and error to try some different combinations?

## Let's solve…

**4** Solve this picture puzzle.

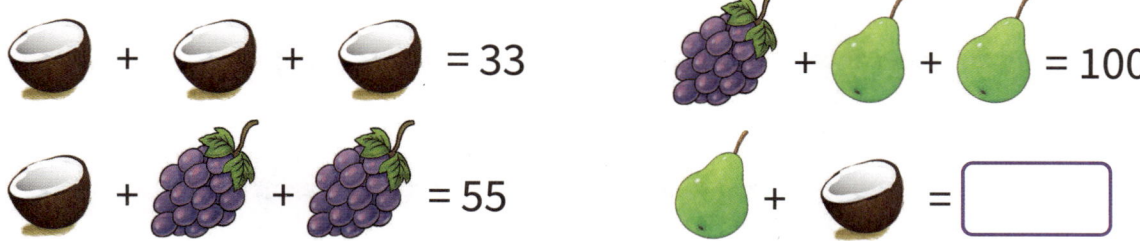

**5** Make up your own picture puzzle for a partner to solve. Use any values between 0 and 500!

 Turn back to page 4 and complete the problem-solving record.

# 5 Migrations

## Let's reason …

**1** Some animals travel long distances at certain times of the year to find food or to breed. These journeys are called **migrations**.

The table gives you information about some different animal migrations.

| Animal | Migration route | Approximate round trip distance (km) |
|---|---|---|
| Green turtle | Brazil – Ascension Island | 4000 |
| Leatherback turtle | Various routes | 16 000 |
| Monarch butterfly | Northern USA and Canada – Mexico | 6400 |
| Arctic tern | Arctic – Antarctica | 59 200 |
| Brent goose | UK – Canada and Greenland | 6000 |
| Grey whale | North Pacific – Mexico | 10 000 |
| Humpback whale | Various routes | 8050 |
| Wildebeest | Circular route in East Africa | 800 |

Discuss questions **a** and **b** with your partner.

**a** Why are migration distances only approximations?

**b** What does the term 'round trip' mean?

Write your answers to questions **c** and **d**.

**c** Which animal has the longest migration route? How far does this animal travel on the outward part of its migration?

_____

**d** Many animals stop along their migration routes to feed. A group of humpback whales stops $\frac{2}{3}$ of the way along their return route. How far have they travelled?

_____

**2** Scientists tracked one flock of Arctic terns. They discovered that the flock travelled a total distance of 25 700 km in 40 days.

**a** Calculate the average distance the flock covered per day.

_____

**b** Estimate the average speed of the birds in km/h for the whole trip.

_____

**3** Marc, Nina, Ani, Li and Sobia discussed which animal migrations interest them most. They chose these five animals:

| whale | tern | wildebeest | butterfly | turtle |

Use the clues to work out who chose each animal.

The name of Nina's animal has an even number of letters.

Marc chose an animal with the same first letter as Nina's.

Ani and Li chose animals that do not have the same first letter.

The name of Sobia's animal has more than 6 letters.

Li and Marc both chose animals that can fly.

**4** Brent geese migrate between the United Kingdom and Greenland. They fly approximately 3000 km (one way) on this route.

Use this information to estimate the distance flown by the other birds: red knots, white storks (two routes) and dunlins.

**a** Write your estimates in the boxes.

**b** Tell your partner how you estimated each distance.

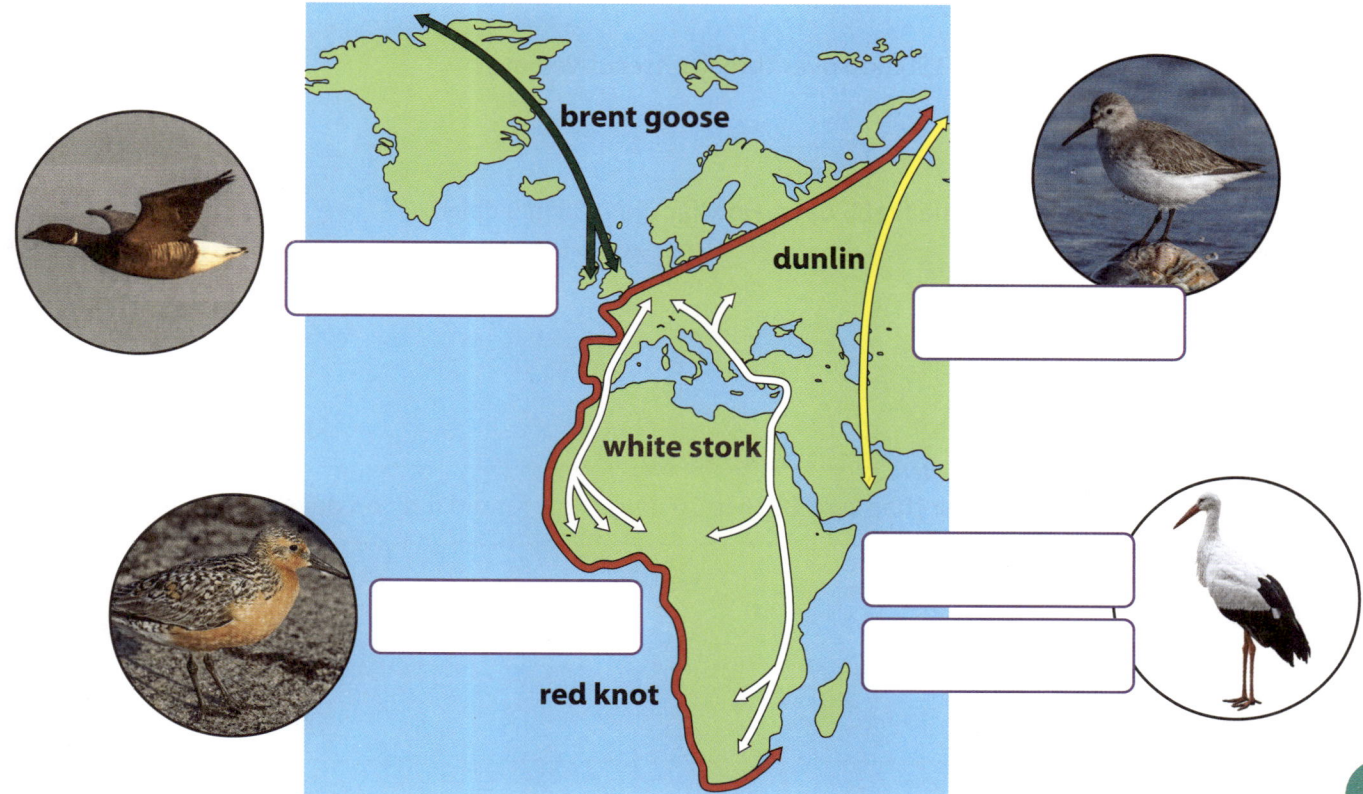

## Let's solve ...

Zara studies black-browed albatrosses to find out how far they fly each day in search of food. She has ringed 5 birds and attached electronic tracking devices to them. The table shows the ring numbers and data about the distance that each bird flew (in km) on each day for 10 days.

**Distances (in kilometres) flown over 10 days**

| Ring number | Day | | | | | | | | | |
|---|---|---|---|---|---|---|---|---|---|---|
| | 1 | 2 | 3 | 4 | 5 | 6 | 7 | 8 | 9 | 10 |
| A103 | 399 | 351 | 299 | 329 | 311 | 380 | 395 | 347 | | |
| B876 | 330 | 345 | 340 | 331 | 337 | 309 | 321 | 339 | 352 | 311 |
| C934 | 350 | 311 | 375 | 315 | 349 | 382 | 305 | 367 | | |
| D122 | 519 | 510 | 495 | 479 | 539 | 481 | 496 | 443 | 527 | |
| E906 | 450 | 422 | 471 | 438 | 467 | 451 | 432 | 504 | 409 | |

**1  a**  Zara calculated how far bird A103 flew in the first two days like this:
Explain what she did.

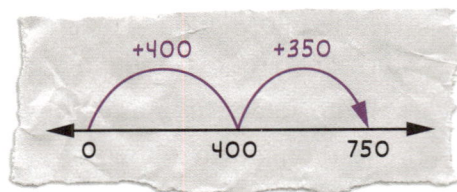

_____

_____

**b**  Which bird flew more than 1500 km over three consecutive days?

_____

**c**  Bird E906 flew 2248 km in the first 5 days. How far did it fly in 9 days?

**d**  Bird C934 flew 12 km further than bird B876 in 10 days. How far did it fly on days 9 and 10?

Birds migrate along routes called flyways. The Central Asian Flyway stretches from Siberia in the north to the Maldives in the south and includes 30 different countries.

**2** 370 species of birds migrate in the Central Asian Flyway. 310 of these species rely on wetlands in the region as their habitat. What percentage of the species do not rely on wetlands?

_____

_____

Central Asian Flyway

**3** Manu tracks the distance that a flock of ducks travelled across the Central Asian Flyway. These are his results for the first four hours.

| Hours | 1 | 2 | 3 | 4 |
|---|---|---|---|---|
| Distance flown (km) | 72 | 96 | 120 | 144 |

**a** What pattern can you see in the data?

_____

**b** Manu stopped tracking the ducks once they had travelled 400 km. Draw a graph to show the relationship between time and distance. Use your graph to estimate how much time Manu spent tracking the ducks.

Assume that the pattern in the data continues in the same way.

## Let's solve …

**1** Most birds need to eat between $\frac{1}{4}$ and $\frac{1}{2}$ of their body mass per day. Work out how much food each of these birds needs per day. Give each answer as a range. Tell your partner how you worked out the answers.

| Bird | Swan | Raven | Sparrow |
|---|---|---|---|
| **Mean mass** | 8.9 kg | 1.2 kg | 27 g |
| **Mass of food needed per day** | | | |

**2** The daily energy needs of some different birds are given in the table.

| Bird | Adult mass (grams) | Daily energy needs (calories) |
|---|---|---|
| Duck | 500 | 300 |
| Robin | 77 | 72 |
| Hummingbird | 3 | 25 |
| Raven | 1200 | 420 |

**a** Do larger birds need more food? Give evidence for your answer.

_____

_____

> What is the ratio of body mass to daily energy needs for each bird?

**b** What does your answer to part **a** tell you about how much energy hummingbirds use each day compared to the other birds?

_____

**c** How does the information for the raven in this table compare with your answers to question 1?

_____

_____

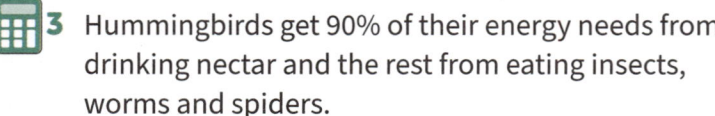

**3** Hummingbirds get 90% of their energy needs from drinking nectar and the rest from eating insects, worms and spiders.

**a** Wildflower nectar has 85 calories per 100 g. How much nectar does a hummingbird need to drink to get 90% of its daily energy needs?

_____

**b** 12 small crickets provide 121 calories. How many crickets does a hummingbird need to eat to get the rest of its daily energy needs?

_____

**4** Gardeners often make 'hummingbird nectar' and place it in feeders for hummingbirds. To make 'hummingbird nectar', they mix sugar and water in the ratio 1 : 4.

**a** Calculate the amount of sugar needed to fill a 250 ml feeder bottle. Show your working.

_____

**b** Sandra has 38 g of sugar. How much water should she mix with it to make hummingbird nectar?

_____

**5** On their migration route, some hummingbirds cross the ocean in the Gulf of Mexico. The shortest route they can take is 800 km long and there is nowhere they can stop to feed. Scientists wondered if this was possible. They did these calculations:

> Male hummingbird
> Mass 4.5 g, of which 2 g = fat
> 1 g of fat = 9 calories
> Flying consumes 0.69 calories per hour

**a** How many hours can the hummingbird fly using energy from its body fat?

_____

_____

_____

> What do you need to work out first? Which numbers do you need in your calculations? Do you need to multiply or divide?

**b** Hummingbirds fly at an average speed of 40 km/h. Is your answer to part **a** enough time to fly the distance required at that speed? Show how you work out your answer.

## Think, talk, solve

Monarch butterflies migrate south from Canada and the USA to spend the winter months in warmer places. The Oyamel pine forest in Mexico is one place where they spend the winter.

**1** Each year, the World Wide Fund for Nature (WWF) works with organizations in Mexico to estimate the number of butterflies that arrive in Oyamel pine forest.

Discuss these questions with your partner.

**a** Why is it not possible to accurately count the number of butterflies that migrate to the forest each year?

**b** How do you think the WWF estimates the numbers?

**2** Estimates for the numbers of butterflies are given in number of butterflies per hectare. A hectare is an area of $10\,000\,m^2$. On average, there are 21.1 million butterflies per hectare.

**a** The largest population of butterflies was found in 1996–1997. The butterflies covered 18 hectares. Work out the approximate size of this population.

_____

**b** The lowest recorded population was in 2013–2014, when the butterflies covered 0.67 hectares. Work out the approximate size of this population.

_____

**c** If there are 21.1 million butterflies in a hectare, how many are there in one square metre?

_____

_____

**3** The diagram shows where the butterflies migrate from.

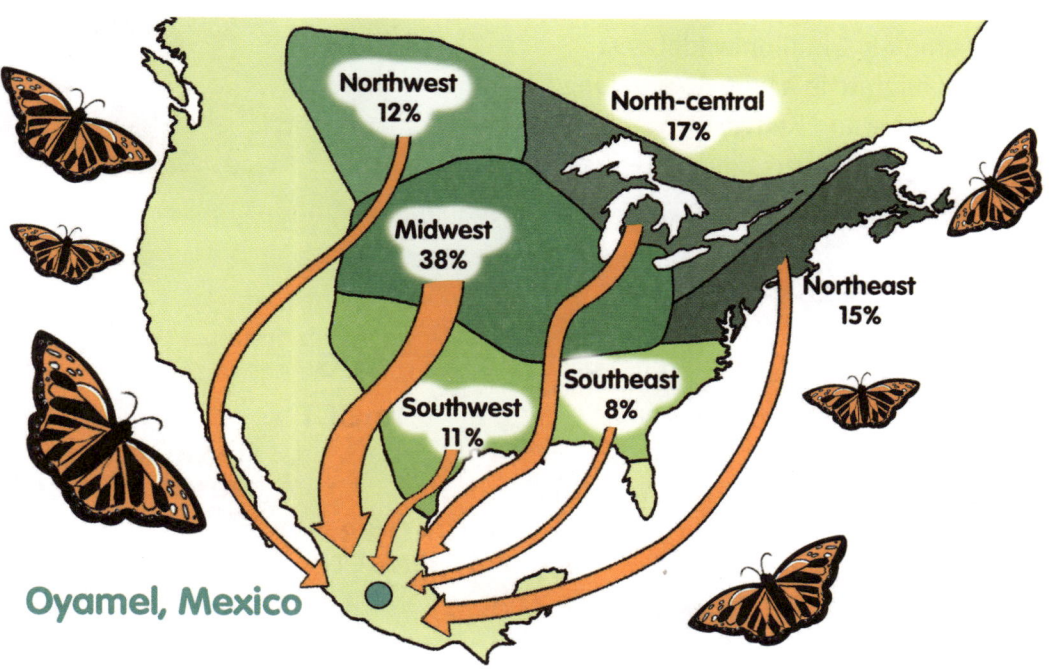

**a** From which region does the greatest **proportion** of the butterflies come?

_____

**b** Which two regions account for half of the butterflies?

_____

**4** In one year, 250 million butterflies migrated to Oyamel.

**a** How many of them migrated from the North-central region?

_____

**b** 96–98% of the migrating butterflies successfully arrived in Oyamel. Calculate how many arrived from the Southeast region. Give your answer as a range.

_____

_____

**5 a** Make up an easy question and a challenging question for your partner to solve using information from these two pages.

Easy: _____

Challenging: _____

**b** Compare and discuss your questions. What makes a question easy for you? What makes it challenging?

## Think, talk, write

Each year approximately 2 million wildebeest, zebra and gazelles migrate in a loop 800 km long across parts of Tanzania and Kenya.

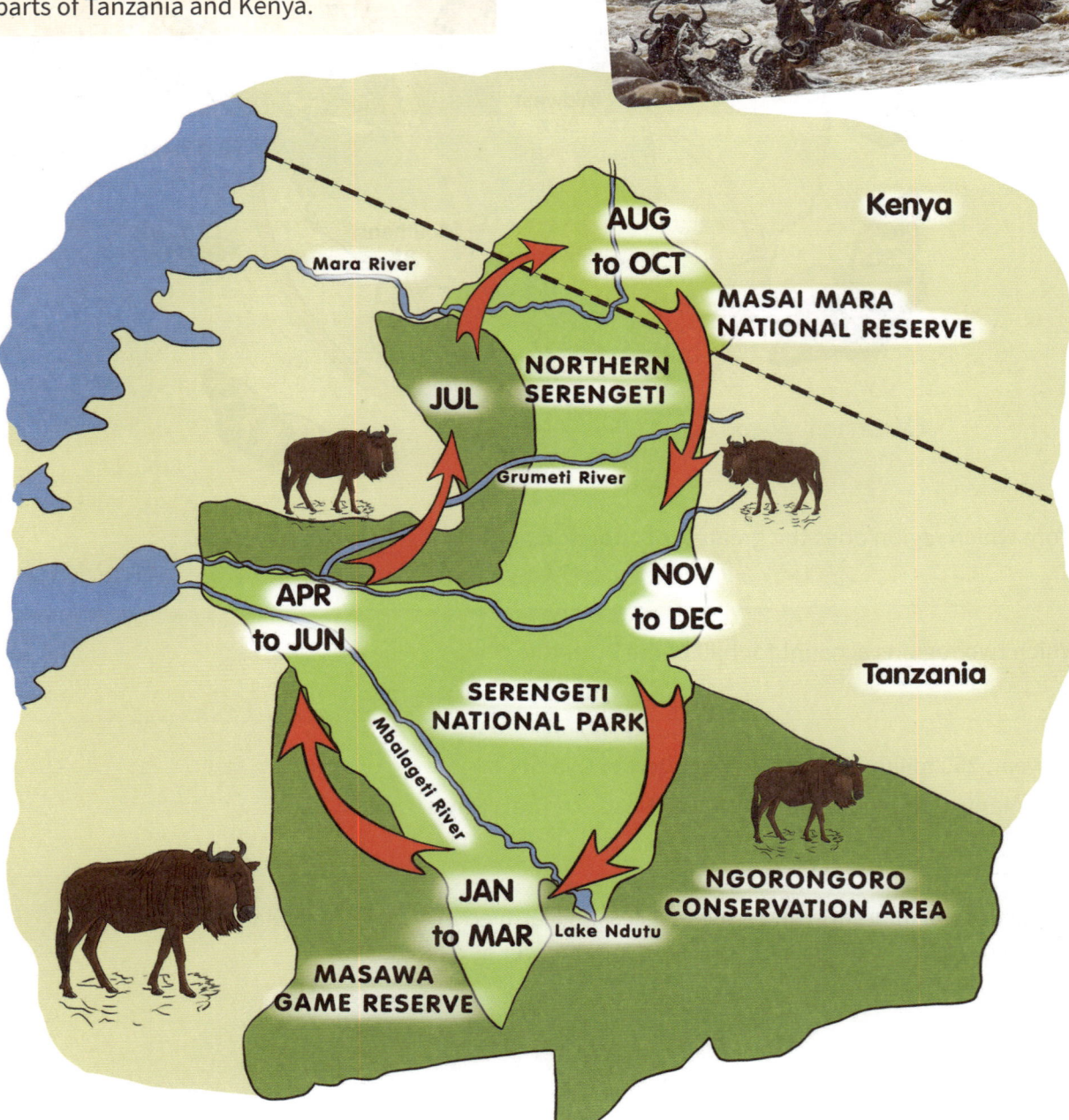

1 Discuss these questions in your group.

a Many tourists visit the national parks to see the wildebeest crossing the Mara River to get to the Masai Mara National Reserve. What time of year is likely to be best for this?

b Where and when could a tourist see other river crossings?

c The wildebeest give birth to their calves in February and March each year. Where is the herd likely to be at this time of year?

d What fraction of the year do the herds spend in Kenya?

**2** In one year, 2.1 million animals take part in the migration. Approximately 1.5 million are wildebeest, 300 000 are zebra and the rest are different types of gazelle.

**a** What percentage of the total animals are wildebeest?

_____

**b** What is the ratio of zebra to wildebeest?

_____

**c** Approximately 1.6% to 2% of the animals do not complete the migration route due to injury or being eaten by predators on the route. Estimate how many wildebeest, zebra and gazelles do not complete the route. Give each answer as a range.

Wildebeest: _____

Zebra: _____

Gazelles: _____

**d** There are 12 major crossing sites on the Mara River. What is the mean number of animals that cross at each site?

_____

**3** Approximately 8000 wildebeest calves are born each day during the calving season. How many are born during a 4-week period?

_____

_____

**4** During the calving season, the probability of seeing a cheetah hunt is 0.85

**a** What is the probability that you will <u>not</u> see a cheetah hunt during the calving season?

_____

**b** If 1500 tourists visit the reserve during the calving season, how many of them are likely to see a cheetah hunt?

_____

**5** On average, wildebeest are about 1.35 m tall at shoulder height, with a body length of 2.4 m and a mass of approximately 200 kg. Zebra are about 1.5 m at shoulder height. They have a body length of 2.3 m and weigh between 250 and 300 kg.

Which animal is bigger? Support your answer mathematically.

_____

_____

## Let's reason …

**1** Loggerhead sea turtles migrate long distances between feeding areas and the beaches where mature females lay their eggs. Female turtles lay eggs only once every 2–3 years. Males and young turtles never come ashore.

Answer these questions with a partner.

**a** Why it is impossible for scientists to work out accurate population numbers of sea turtles?

**b** Newly hatched turtles migrate back to feeding areas. How do you think they know where to go?

**2** Every 14 days, female turtles leave the water and go onto the beach at night to lay eggs. They lay 4 clutches of eggs with 100 to 120 eggs in each.

The number of females in three of the main breeding areas are:

> A clutch is a group of eggs laid together.

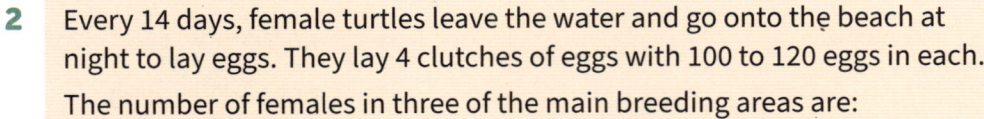

| Florida (USA) 20 000 | Oman 13 000 | Japan and Eastern Australia 1200 |

**a** Estimate the length of time females stay near the beaches where they lay their eggs.

_____

**b** Approximately how many eggs does each female lay?

_____

**c** Calculate the number of turtle eggs on the beaches of Oman if each female lays 4 clutches of 120 eggs.

_____

**d** Scientists estimate that only 1 in 1000 baby turtles that reach the ocean survive to maturity (30 years) and that 7.6% of hatchlings do not make it into the ocean after they hatch.

> A hatchling is a baby turtle that has just hatched from its egg.

Assume 95% of the eggs on the beaches of Oman hatch. Estimate how many turtles reach the water and how many of those grow to maturity.

> Use the number you worked out for Oman in part **c**.

**3** The table gives data about the migration of four tracked whales off the coast of Alaska (USA). Work out and fill in all the missing data.

Include both the start and end dates when you work out the number of days tracked.

| Whale tag number | 2023 migration start date | Date of last data collected | Number of days tracked | Total distance migrated (km) | Mean daily distance migrated (km) |
|---|---|---|---|---|---|
| A865 | 25 Nov | | 31 | | 141 |
| B3221 | 2 Dec | 8 Jan 2024 | | 4775 | |
| C098 | 19 Nov | 13 Dec 2023 | | | 146.3 |
| D399 | 28 Nov | | 46 | 4303 | |

**4** In 2015 scientists tracked a female grey whale, which swam from Russia to Mexico and back. The whale travelled 22 380 km in 172 days. What was the whale's average swimming speed?

**5** This chart shows the number of whale sightings off the coast of the USA for the first four months of the year.

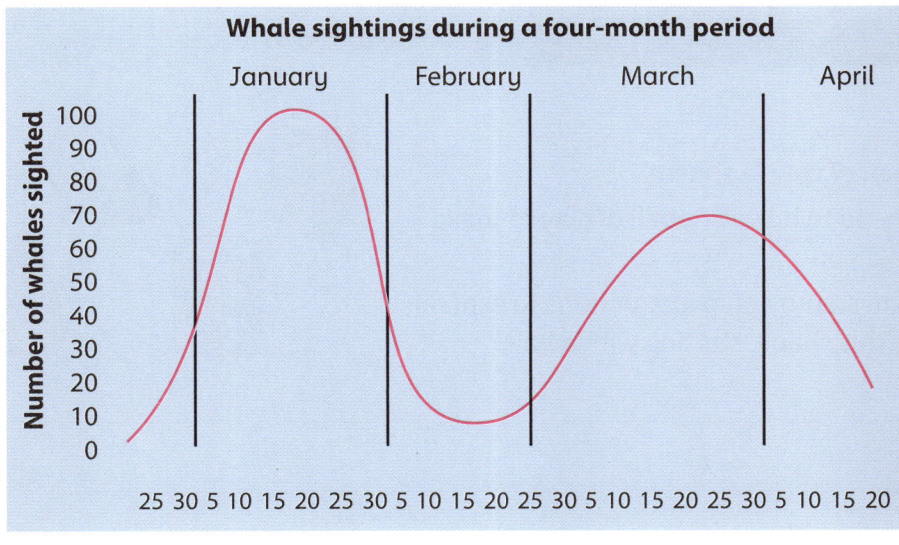

Whale sightings during a four-month period

January   February   March   April

Number of whales sighted

25 30 5 10 15 20 25 30 5 10 15 20 25 30 5 10 15 20 25 30 5 10 15 20

Write three questions for your partner to answer using the data shown. Each question should involve a different type of maths.

_____

_____

_____

➡ Turn back to page 4 and complete the problem-solving record.

## Think, talk, reason

1 Siv works in a pottery studio. Pottery is the name we give to objects made from clay, such as bowls, plates, cups and vases. Look at the photograph and discuss these questions with a partner.

What 3D shapes do you notice in the objects on the shelves and table?

How are they similar or different to the 3D shapes you have learned about (spheres, cubes, cylinders, cones and prisms)?

Talk about what you think each type of object might be used for. How is its shape suited to its use?

2 All the pottery items begin life as a ball of clay (a sphere).

   a Discuss with a partner what you need to do with a ball of clay to make each of these 3D shapes.

   b Choose one of the 3D shapes. Write step-by-step instructions to explain to a Stage 2 student how to make this shape, starting with a ball.

First... _____

_____

Next... _____

_____

Then... _____

_____

Discuss your instructions with your partner.

## Let's solve...

The raw clay comes in 12.5 kg bags. Siv keeps this guide to remind him how much clay to use when he starts making each type of item.

**3** For each item, calculate how many Siv could make from 1 full bag of clay, and how much clay would be left over.

| Item | Weight |
|---|---|
| Cup/mug | 300 g |
| Small bowl | 450 g |
| Soup bowl | 900 g |
| Serving bowl | 1500 g |
| Side plate | 1000 g |
| Dinner plate | 2000 g |

**a** cups

**b** soup bowls

**c** serving bowls

**4** From one bag of clay, Siv decides to make equal numbers of cups and small bowls. How many of each can he make, and how much clay will he have left over?

**5** Suggest two different combinations of items that Siv could make that would use exactly one whole bag of clay, with none left over.

## Let's solve...

Siv is using a computer program to design some wrapping paper to use in his pottery shop.

**1 a** He enters coordinates to draw a 2D pot shape. You can see the shape on the grid on page 69. The coordinates of point A are (−7, 8). Write the coordinates of the other points.

B _____    C _____

D _____    E _____

F _____    G _____

H _____

**b** The pot shape has one line of symmetry. Choose 3 points on the mirror line and write their coordinates. What do you notice about the coordinate pairs? Can you explain this?

_____

_____

 **2** For the wrapping paper design, Siv uses the pot shape to create a repeating pattern. He wants to arrange the pots in vertical columns, with 2 units (blocks) of space between the shapes.

The first two coordinates of the next shape in the pattern are $A_1$ (−7, 1) and $B_1$ (−3, 1).

**a** Plot the remaining points and draw the shape in its new position. Label the points $C_1$, $D_1$ and so on.

**b** Tick the possible instructions that Siv gave the drawing program to make the pot shape.
There may be more than one correct answer.

> When you transform a shape, for example by reflecting or translating it, you give each point on the new shape a subscript number.

reflect in the mirror line ☐

slide down 7 units ☐

reflect in the $y$-axis ☐

translate −7 along the $y$-axis ☐

translate down 3 and across 4 ☐

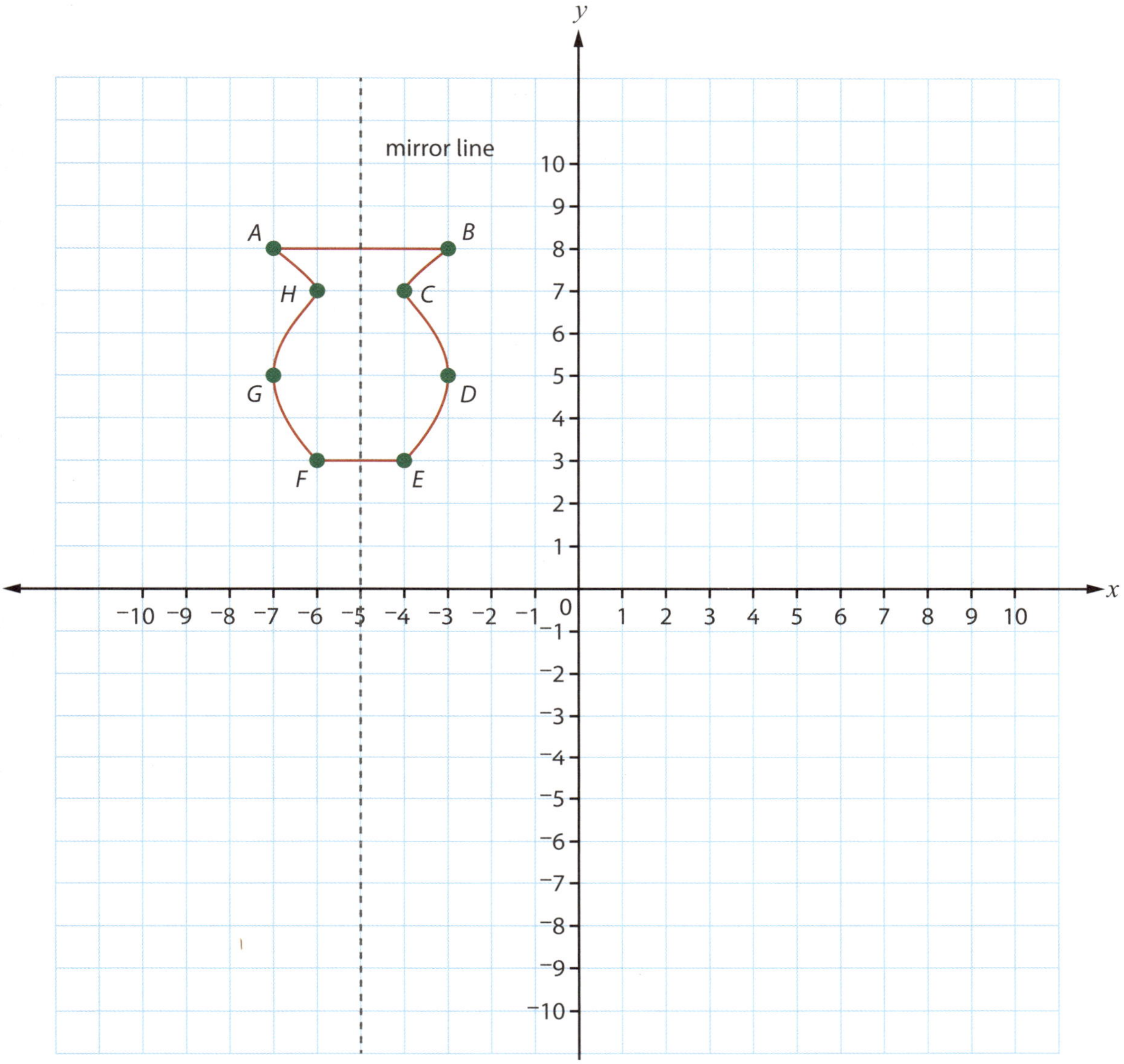

mirror line

*A*  *B*

*H*  *C*

*G*  *D*

*F*  *E*

**3** Siv continues using the drawing program to make this wrapping paper design.

**a** Work with a partner. Decide on two more positions for the pot shape on the coordinate grid that will help to create the pattern.

**b** Draw your new shapes on the grid and label the coordinates.

Remember to label the points correctly. Use subscript $_2$ and subscript $_3$ for each shape.

### Read, think, reason

While the clay is still fresh and wet, the potter can shape and mould it. The wetter the clay, the softer it is. As clay dries, it hardens. When most of the water has dried from the clay, the pots are fired in a kiln. This dries and hardens the clay even more.

**1** This table summarizes the main states of clay. Some information is missing. Use the descriptions below to help you complete the table.

| State of clay | Clay percentage | Water percentage |
|---|---|---|
| Slip | | |
| Plastic clay | | |
| | | 10% |
| | 98% | |
| | | 0% |

Slip is a mixture that is about half clay, half water. The potter can pour slip into a mould or use it like a glue to stick one piece of clay to another.

Mostly, the potter works with clay in a plastic state. It is soft enough to mould, but not mushy. At this stage, it is about $\frac{1}{4}$ water and $\frac{3}{4}$ clay.

As the clay dries out, its state changes to leather hard. In this state, the potter can still smooth the clay and carve into the surface, but trying to mould the main shape would cause the clay to crack. Leather hard clay is about $\frac{1}{10}$ water.

Finally, the clay is bone-dry. This means that it is almost completely dry, and ready to be fired.

After firing, the clay is 100% dry. This state is called bisque. The potter uses a special paint called glaze to decorate and coat the pot. It contains glass that will melt and form a hard, shiny coating.

**2** The percentages in the table are by volume. Which of the following statements are true based on that information?

Write true or false for each statement. Explain your thinking to a partner.

**a** Half a litre of slip contains about 1 cup of water. _____

**b** 2 kg of slip contains about 1 kg of clay. _____

**c** 10 cubic centimetres of leather hard clay contains about 1 cubic centimetre of water. _____

## Let's solve ...

**3** A ceramic mug shrinks during drying and firing, losing 10% of its original height.
The original height of the mug was 125 mm. What is the new height?

**4** The mass of a wet clay plate is 430 g. It loses 8% of its mass during drying and firing. What is the mass of the finished plate?

**5** Siv mixes smooth red clay with brown clay in a 2 : 3 ratio by mass. He needs a total of 600 g of clay for this project. How many grams of each clay should he use?

## Think, talk, reason

1 Discuss the photograph with a partner.

- What shapes and angles do you notice?

- Think of the words we use to describe parts of circles: centre, radius, diameter, angle. Try to use these words to describe what you see.

- The design for each plate started as a blank circle. What do you think the designer did first to create each design?

- What did the designer have to measure?

- How could using fractions help the designer?

2 The angles around a point add up to 360°. In each of these plates, all the angles around the centre point are equal.

Plate A

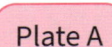

Plate B

Plate C

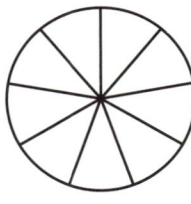

Plate D

Use your understanding of circles and angles to help you calculate the size of the angles on each plate.

> You don't need to measure the angles.

|  | Plate A | Plate B | Plate C | Plate D |
|---|---|---|---|---|
| Size of each angle around the centre |  |  |  |  |

3 The designer uses one of the four plates in question 2 to create a different design where each angle is $\frac{1}{3}$ of a right angle.

a Which plate does she use?

b What is the smallest number of lines she has to draw on this plate to create the new design?

## Let's reason …

Many plate designs use **concentric** circles. Concentric circles have the same centre point but different radii.

How can you use the diagrams to help you solve these problems?

**4** A plate has a 26 cm diameter. The designer wants to create a circular border that is 6 cm wide. What is the radius of the inner concentric circle she should draw on her plate?

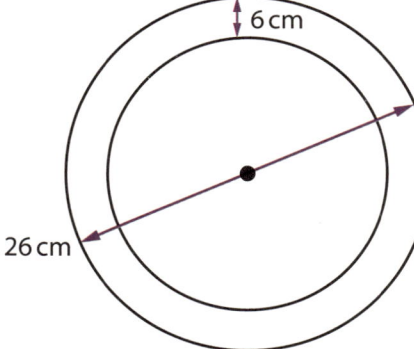

**5** Another plate is 30 cm in diameter. The designer wants to draw concentric circles to create this design. She wants all the rings to be of equal thickness. Explain how she should measure and draw the circles.

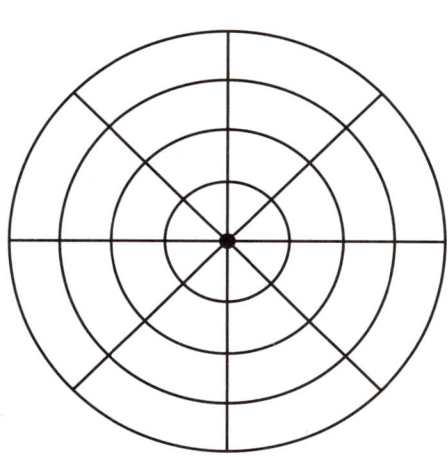

**6 a** Design your own plate. Write a description of the shapes and angles you used.

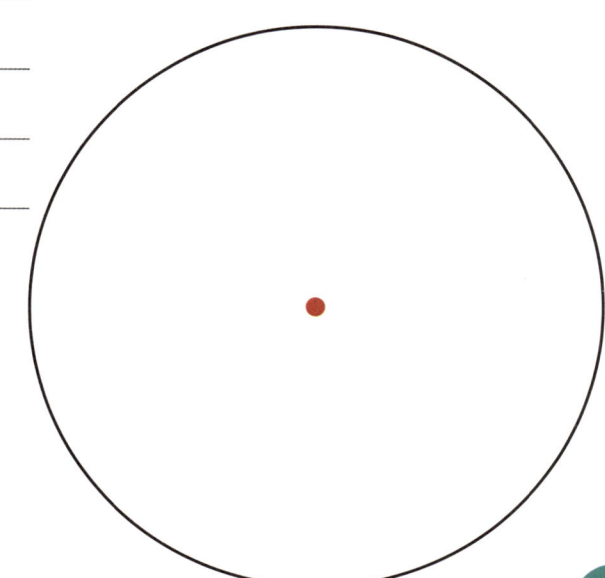

**b** Share your designs in a group. Discuss the different shapes and angles you used. What are the similarities and differences?

### Think, talk, write

Julie made these notes about the temperature of her kiln when she fired her pots.

- When I put the pots in, the kiln was at room temperature: 20 °C.
- I turned on the kiln.
- After 1 hour, the temperature reached 250 °C.
- It reached 700 °C an hour later, and I turned down the dial.
- The temperature dropped by 80 °C within half an hour, and then another 120 °C over the next half hour.
- It was at 410 °C by the four-hour mark, and dropped another 100 °C an hour later than that.
- I left the door closed for another five hours, and the temperature slowly came back down to room temperature before I opened it again.

1  Use this grid to draw a line graph showing how the temperature of Julie's kiln changed from the start to the end of the firing time.

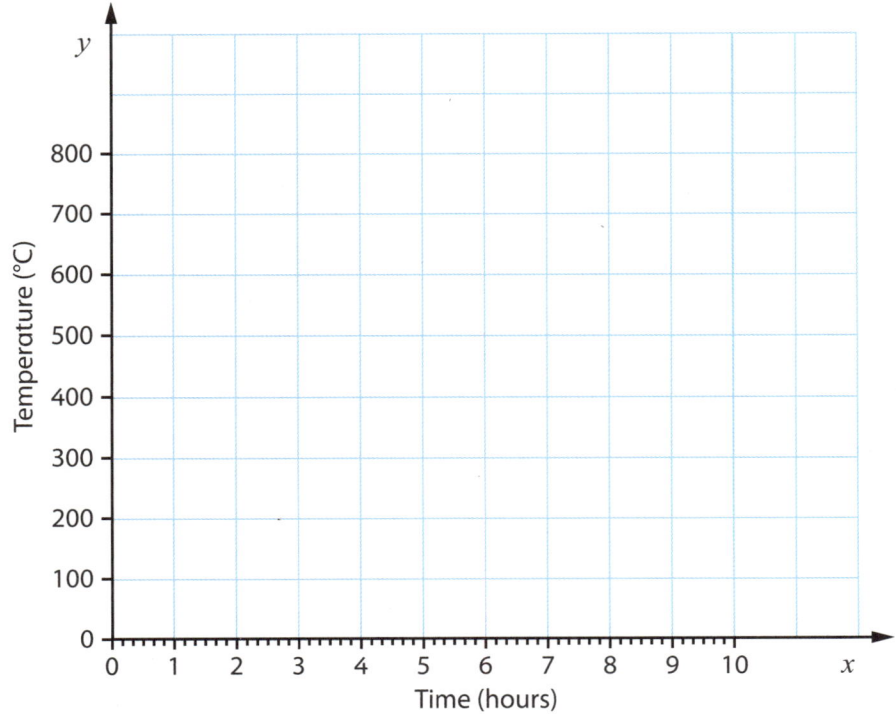

## Let's reason …

**2**  Why did the temperature not begin at zero, but the time did begin at zero?

_____

**3**  Julie turned on the kiln at 8:45 a.m.

   **a**  At what time did the kiln reach its highest temperature?  _____

   **b**  At what time did Julie open the kiln after the firing?  _____

**4**  Identify the top and bottom temperatures reached by Julie's kiln. Use these to determine the range of the temperatures.

> Remember, the range of a data set is the difference between the smallest value and the greatest value.

**5**  The temperature changed at an average rate of:

- 230°C/h in the first hour
- 340°C/h in the first two hours
- 200°C/h in the third hour.

Explain how <u>all</u> these statements can be true.

_____

_____

**6**  A kiln is at 100°C, and the temperature increases steadily at a rate of 25°C every 20 minutes. How long will it take to reach 900°C?

## Timeline of important developments in the history of pottery

**29 000–25 000 BCE**
Ancient communities in the Czech Republic made figurines of animals and people from clay.

**18 000–17 000 BCE**
The earliest known examples of Chinese pottery are from this period. Artefacts have been found in Jiangxi.

**13 000 BCE**
Japanese people of the Jomon era made unglazed pots.

**9500 BCE**
Pottery-making began in Mali.

**6300 BCE**
Pottery-making began in ancient Greece.

**3500 BCE**
The invention of the potter's wheel allowed potters to create smooth, round pots.

**600 CE**
The high-temperature kiln was invented in China. These kilns reached a temperature of 1350 °C. Potters could now fire white porcelain (fine white clay).

**1400s CE**
Blast furnaces were invented in Europe to melt metals. They reached a temperature of 1500 °C.

**1300s–1600s CE**
The Ming Dynasty in China produced world-famous blue and white Ming porcelain.

## Let's solve ...

**1 a** How long ago did people start making pottery? Circle the best answer.

> A century is a period of 100 years.
> A millennium is a period of 1000 years.

| about 30 centuries ago | about 2 millennia ago | about 30 millennia ago |

**b** How did you work this out?

_____

_____

**2 a** Approximately how much time passed between the time of the very earliest known clay figurines, and the first Chinese pottery from Jiangxi? Circle the best answer.

| about 5000 years | about 10 millennia | about 17 millennia |

**b** Explain to a partner how you worked it out.

**3** How much older is a Czech figurine made in 28 500 BCE than a Ming vase made in 1550 CE?

**4** Imagine you have a time machine. You travel to the time when the Chinese invented the high-temperature kiln.

**a** How far back in time did you have to travel from the present?

**b** How many more years do you have to go back in time to reach the time when people invented the potter's wheel?

**c** You use your time machine to travel to an archaeological dig taking place in 1927. One of the pots found at the site is 12 500 years old. In what year was it made?

→ Turn back to page 4 and complete the problem-solving record.

# Glossary

**baseline** a starting point

**concentric** describing circles that have the same centre point but different radii. Concentric circles are the curved equivalent of parallel lines, as they never meet.

**consecutive** following one after the other

**cumulative** adding up over time

**debt** money that is owed. To be in debt means to owe money.

**dimension** the length, width or height of an object. Dimensions are all lengths that we can measure.

**donation** something given to a charity, either as a gift or money

**equation** a mathematical statement showing two values or expressions that are equal. An equation always uses the = sign.

**formula** a relationship or rule expressed using numbers and letters. For example, the formula for the area of a rectangle is L × W, where L represents the length and W represents the width.

$$s = 2 \times b \qquad s = 2 + b \qquad s = b \div 2$$

$s$ = number of pairs of shoes
$b$ = number of pairs boots

**mean** also called average. The mean of a set of values is the sum of the values divided by the number of values. For example, the mean of 10, 12 and 20 = (10 + 12 + 20) ÷ 3 = 14.

**migration** a movement of a large group or population over a long distance

**pledge** promise

**proportion** fraction or part of a whole group. When things are in proportion, the parts relate to each other in a balanced way.

**projection** an estimate or prediction about how a trend will continue in the future

**rearrangement** putting things in a different composition or order

**sponsor** (noun) someone who pays funds towards a project, especially for a charity; (verb) to give a donation to a charity or person

**trend** a pattern or direction